W9-BQX-618

# FIFTEEN WINDS

*A SELECTION OF MODERN CANADIAN POEMS*

*EDITED BY A. W. PURDY*



McGraw-Hill Ryerson Limited
Toronto
Montreal New York London Sydney
Mexico Johannesburg Panama Düsseldorf
Singapore Rio de Janeiro Kuala Lumpur New Delhi

ISBN 0-7700-3175-7 Paper Edition

6 7 8 9 0 D 0 9 8 7 6 5 4



Printed and bound in Canada

# ACKNOWLEDGMENTS

For permission to reprint copyrighted material, grateful acknowledgment is made to the following publishers, authors, and agents:

Milton Acorn for "I've Tasted My Blood", "Callum", "Sky's Poem for Christmas" and "Knowing I Live in a Dark Age."

Margaret Atwood for "Dreams of the Animals."

Earle Birney for "Mammoth Corridors."

Bill Bissett for "Nuclear Circular" and "Poem."

George Bowering for "Esta muy caliente" from THE MAN IN YELLOW BOOTS, El Corno Emplumado (Mexico) 1965, and "The Canada Council Poet."

Ivan Burgess for "As He Lay Dying" from FLOWERS OF GRAVE CONCERN, Cameron Press.

City Lights Books for "Christ Walks in this Infernal District Too", "Without the Nighted Wyvern" and "Old Freighter in an Old Port" from SELECTED POEMS OF MALCOLM LOWRY, copyright © 1962 by Margerie Lowry. Reprinted by permission of CITY LIGHTS BOOKS.

Clarke Irwin for "Someone Has to Eat" and "The Trap" from LOST AND FOUND by Raymond H. Souster, published by Clarke, Irwin and Company Ltd., Reproduced by permission.

John Robert Colombo for "The French in Quebec". Reprinted from THE MACKENZIE POEMS by William Lyon Mackenzie and John Robert Colombo (Toronto: Swan Publishing Company, 1966) with permission.

Frank Davey for "The Fact" from BRIDGE FORCE, Contact Press.

Louis Dudek for "Inscriptions" from THE TRANSPARENT SEA, Contact Press.

R. G. Everson for "When I'm Going Well" from A LATTICE FOR MOMOS, Contact Press and the SATURDAY REVIEW, New York.

Doug Fetherling for "Night Before Last."

The Canadian Forum for "Song for Conformists" by Kildare Dobbs; "Cold-water Flat Blues" by Len Gasparini; "The Nu Nollej" by Derek Pethick; "Apologies to Robert Frost" by W. W. E. Ross; "Neanderthal National Anthem" by F. E. Sparshott; "The Dow Recruiter" and "The Season of Eden" by Tom Wayman.

Eldon Grier for "Tony at Sea" and "Bury Me in My Cadillac" from POEMS, privately printed.

George Jonas for "Peace" from THE ABSOLUTE SMILE, House of Anansi.

Patrick Lane for "Elephants" from THE CORRUGATED I by Patrick Lane; "Portrait" from THE CIRCUS IN THE BOY'S EYES, Very Stone House, by Jim Brown; and for "On Reading a Poem Written in Adolescence", Very Stone House by Pat Lowther.

Dennis Lee for "400: Coming Home" and "He Asks Her."

McClelland and Stewart for "The Bear on the Delhi Road", "Twenty Third Flight", "Canada: Case History", and "Meeting of Strangers" from SELECTED POEMS by Earle Birney; for "Composition in Late Spring", "How Poems Get Written", "The Satyr", "On Seeing the Statuettes of Ezekiel and Jeremiah in the Church of Notre Dame" and "To the Girls of my Graduating Class" from COLLECTED POEMS by Irving Layton; for "Old Alex", "Percy Lawson", "Hockey Players" and "Interruption" from CARIBOO HORSES by A. W. Purdy; for "Drunk Tank" and "On Being a

Member of the Armed Forces" from WILD GRAPE VINE by A. W. Purdy; and for "E.P.J." from FLOWERS FOR HITLER by Leonard Cohen. Reprinted by permission of The Canadian Publishers, McClelland and Stewart Limited, Toronto.

Annette and Jim Murray for "Benoit" from the record Melbourne (Rodeo) AMLP 4005.

Music Publishers Holding Corp. for "Four Strong Winds" by Ian Tyson. Copyright 1963 by M. Witmark & Sons. Used by permission.

John Newlove for "Then, If I Cease Desiring", "The Flowers", and "A Letter to Larry Sealey" from MOVING IN ALONE, Contact Press; and for "Not Moving" from ELEPHANTS, MOTHERS AND OTHERS, Periwinkle Press.

The New Yorker Magazine for "War on the Periphery" by George Johnston. Copr. © 1951 The New Yorker Magazine, Inc. Reprinted by permission.

Alden Nowlan for "In the Hainesville Cemetery" from A DARKNESS IN THE EARTH, Hearse Press; "Lament for James Talbot" from Queens Quarterly Summer 1959; for "Street Corner Idler" and "I Knew the Seasons Ere I Knew the Hours" from WIND IN A ROCKY COUNTY, Emblem Books and for "The Bull Moose", and "The Execution" from THE THINGS WHICH ARE, Contact Press.

Oxford University Press for "Campers" by Robert Finch; for "The Lonely Land" and "To Hold in a Poem" from COLLECTED POEMS by A. J. M. Smith; for "At the Tourist Center in Boston" and "Backdrop Addresses Cowboy" from THE ANIMALS IN THAT COUNTRY by Margaret Atwood; and for "The Roll Call" from THE CRUISING AUK by George Johnston.

James Reaney for "Klaxon". Reprinted from THE RED HEART AND OTHER POEMS by James Reaney by permission of the author.

Joe Rosenblatt for "Waiter! There's an Alligator in My Coffee", and "The Work Shift" from THE LSD LEACOCK, Coach House Press.

The Ryerson Press for "Islanders" and "El Cortijo" from THE BRAIN'S THE TARGET by Milton Acorn; for "Appointment" from POINTING by Lionel Kearns; for "Frigidaire" and "Political Meeting" from THE ROCKING CHAIR AND OTHER POEMS by A. M. Klein; for "Snow Story" from VIPERS BUGLOSS by L. A. Mackay; for "Saturday Night", "The Gift" and "Nancy" from UNDER THE ICE by Alden Nowlan; for "Five Per Cent" from COMPLETE POEMS by Robert Service; for "Flight of the Roller Coaster", "The Victory", "The Top Hat", "The Introduction", "The Lake of Bays", "When it comes my turn", "The Burial", "The Wind", and "Freeze-up" from THE COLOUR OF THE TIMES by Raymond Souster.

Mrs. Duncan Campbell Scott for "The Forsaken" by Duncan Campbell Scott.

F. R. Scott for "Examiner" and "Laurentian Shield" from SELECTED POEMS by F. R. Scott, Oxford Press.

Peter Stevens for "Warming Up, Tuning In".

A. Szumigalski for "Victim", from THE FIDDLEHEAD, Spring 1968.

Ian Young for "Fear of the Landscape", from T. O. NOW, House of Anansi.

Every reasonable precaution has been taken to trace the owners of copyrighted material and to make due acknowledgment. Any omissions will be gladly rectified in future editions.

# INTRODUCTION

This collection started out to be an anthology designed for schools, and it is still that. But in choosing the poems I found I was selecting only those that I liked, with very little regard for the possible age of the reader. In short, I was compiling a collection of my favourite poems, a rather different thing from compiling an anthology that sets out to be representative of every historical period and offend no one. This collection represents my own particular taste, which I believe will also appeal to other people.

As a possible concession to younger age groups, I did not include poems whose primary object (apart from "Snow Story") seems to be to puzzle the reader, or poems of such a heavy mythological content that they sink almost immediately beneath the surface of the reader's memory. Such poems are not my favourites anyway, and they may be found in other collections for readers who are interested in them.

The reason for the book being in existence at all is the self-evident fact that poetry has changed greatly over the past twenty years. Self-evident only in the poetry itself, for this change has not been adequately reflected in school anthologies. These still contain fossil remnants in the form of poems whose language, even at the time of writing, was never the natural speech of living people. But then I can't conceive of real human beings talking in the stilted language of some poems written as recently as thirty years ago.

There are three exceptions to this rule of including only modern poems: Lampman's "Morning on the Lievre" and Lanigan's "A Threnody" are both nineteenth century. But I regard the former as a near-perfect lyric and the latter as simply too hilarious to leave out for any reason. D. C. Scott's "The Forsaken" was probably written some time after the turn of the century, and strikes me as good no matter what its period of writing.

Language in poems has changed greatly in the last twenty years. The identity and occupations of poets themselves have also changed. (Poets are no longer exclusively university professors or ladies in literary gossip groups who read each other's poems about enduring passion between tea and toast. Poets' jobs run to everything from taxi driver to factory worker—and I've been both myself.) Poets are whoever they happen to be—and they happen to be whoever writes good poems. In short, to be a poet is not to belong to some form of intellectual aristocracy: anybody can do it who can do it.

In some degree the aim and intent of poetry itself has changed. At one time poems talked about "beauty" in vague mystical terms, and described "truth" in an agony of mystic adoration. (Bliss Carman is a good example of this kind of poet.) Today's poetry talks about today's world, topics you're liable to run into on the street or read in the morning paper. Also, of course, it treats things that are timeless. Love, death, and birth are timeless, for instance: but the incidents that compose life are transient as is the individual life itself. Some things are both: laughter is both transitory in the individual and timeless in the human race.

But I started out to say that today's subjects for poems may be anything. Human emotions have reference to all things contained in the human world, whether a door knob or a kitchen faucet (and I've written about both). An English poet named Davies once said "A rainbow and a cuckoo's song may never come together again." Neither would have come together in the first place if a poet hadn't seen the connection. In fact I can't think of anything that hasn't been written about in poems, any object, that is. The inter-relations of human emotions are something else: many of those are still a mystery.

Among the things I don't believe in are long introductions, and this isn't going to be one. Some comments on the poems (which I think ought to be read only after the poems themselves have been read and talked about) are necessary for this kind of book, and anything I want to say, perhaps too much in some cases, has been said in the notes. The poems in this book are good ones—I believe by any standards except out-of-date nonsense. Most of them are my personal favourites. I hope you enjoy them too.

A. W. PURDY

My thanks to Ivan Burgess for help and advice.

# CONTENTS

# POEMS

# *Milton Acorn*

## ISLANDERS

Would you guess from their broad greeting,
witty tuck of eyelids,
how they putt-putt out with lunch-cans
on a sea liable to tangle
and dim out the land between two glances?

Tho their dads toed the decks of schooners,
dodging the blustery rush of capes,
and rum-runner uncles used wit-grease
against the shoot-first Yankee cutters,
they wouldn't be the kind to sail their
                    lobster-boats around the world
for anything less than a dollar-ninety an hour.

## I'VE TASTED MY BLOOD

If this brain's over-tempered
consider that the fire was want
and the hammers were fists.
I've tasted my blood too much
to love what I was born to.

But my mother's look
was a field of brown oats, soft-bearded;
her voice rain and air rich as lilacs:
and I loved her too much to like
how she dragged her days like a sled over gravel.

Playmates? I remember where their skulls roll!
One died hungry, gnawing grey porch-planks;
one fell, and landed so hard he splashed;
and many and many
come up atom by atom
in the worm-casts of Europe.

My deep prayer a curse.
My deep prayer the promise that this won't be.
My deep prayer my cunning,
my love, my anger,
and often even my forgiveness
that this won't be and be.
I've tasted my blood too much
to abide what I was born to.

## "CALLUM"

IN MEMORY OF A NOVICE MINER

He had hair like mustard-weed;
shoulders a scoop;
eyes a lake you see the rocks on bottom;
and his voice swung a loop
with music in what it said
that tangled inside your head.

"Callum" was his name
—pronounced as if he'd sign it on the sun.
From "The Island" he came:
don't know which one.

We dropped to work in our cage,
hearts somewhere behind on a parachute.
That pusher was cute
—saw him a guy who'd count doing right important,
put him at a hard job beside a well
. . . a hundred and forty feet,
and he fell.

Look anywhere:
at buildings bumping on clouds,
at spider-grill bridges:
you'll see no plaque or stone for men killed there:
  but on the late shift
the drill I'm bucking bangs his name in code
. . . "Callum";
tho where "The Island" is I'll never know.

## SKY'S POEM FOR CHRISTMAS

As from milky vapour, dust of atoms jostling like hornets,
a nebula swigs great swatches of itself into a new sun
raw with light, ravener to its parent mists, messenger
to far astronomers thirsty for the word, the word
that'll unlock them: I've never lost a faith
or wrenched my roots of eyes from the heart . . .
Each doom to joy and torment's nourished
within my old love, becomes a new focus
pulsing radiation, disrupting
the foggy smut of death about it;
while I still step to the blood's rhythm,
the soul's reason in those old stories
of kings and white-hot new stars, wonderful babes
like Jupiter's yowl making that Island cave boom like an organ,
born to laugh a challenge at the old cruel gods.

Surely at least once when a new star burst thru heaven
three old men foresook the stern fantasies
of mummy-clothes they'd wrapped around the world,
and surely they found at least one babe
who held great bear time by its short tail . . .
For birth by birth the many-colored creatures of Earth
break ranks and dance apart calling their names and numbers
to reassemble with shouting and elbow-digs
in formations first seen by the mindseye of a child.

Christmas I became that ho-ho-ho of a saint
to wind on a balky piebald disbelieving burro
along the wisemen's trail thru a desert of grown-up people
like cactus with its growth stalled in tormented poses:
til housed and run around by squirrels I found the boy Sky
with eyes hazel windows into outré dimensions
now looking out on wonder, now looking in
at wonder . . . I came not with gifts but
for a present of the universe made strange, tumbling
with odd fuzzy animals, blue of high heaven
siphoned down to tank up my brain,
for meteors he caught and sent sizzling past my ears:
And for myself made quaint, totemic
like a thick oak come wobbling, walking
grotesquely on its roots over patches of dark and sunlight.

## KNOWING I LIVE IN A DARK AGE

Knowing I live in a dark age before history,
I watch my wallet and
am less struck by gunfights in the avenues
than by the newsie with his dirty pink chapped face
calling a shabby poet back for his change.

The crows mobbing the blinking, sun-stupid owl;
wolves eating a hamstrung calf hindend first,
keeping their meat alive and fresh . . . these
are marks of foresight, beginnings of wit:
but Jesus wearing thorns and sunstroke
beating his life and death into words
to break the rods and blunt the axes of Rome;
this and like things followed.

Knowing that in this advertising rainbow
I live like a trapeze artist with a headache,
my poems are no aspirins . . . they show
pale bayonets of grass waving thin on dunes;
the paralytic and his lyric secrets;
my friend Al, union builder and cynic,
hesitating to believe his own delicate poems
lest he believe in something better than himself:
and history, which is yet to begin,
will exceed this, exalt this
as a poem erases and rewrites its poet.

## AT *EL CORTIJO*

At *El Cortijo,* with coffee
tilting right and left
in talk weird as alcohol,
a little dark one backed
into my knee, didn't
look around . . . just sat on it.

No introduction! She took
my femur for a public perch,
and in that exhilarant
fluctuation of conversation
quivered
like a kitten ready to bounce.

I wrung myself with love
for the finely wound nerve of her,
balanced there,
and the way loose hairs
half-twisted
at her palpitating nape.

Disturbed by my rude eye
she twitched round to glare
my grin into a grimace,
then looked back
but didn't budge
her delicate handful of a bum.

---

# *Margaret Atwood*

## DREAMS OF THE ANIMALS

Mostly the animals dream
of other animals   each
according to its kind

(though certain mice and small rodents
have nightmares of a huge pink
shape with five claws descending)

: moles dream of darkness and delicate
mole smells

frogs dream of green and golden
frogs
sparkling like wet suns
among the lilies

red and black
striped fish, their eyes open
have red and black striped
dreams   defence, attack, meaningful
patterns

birds dream of territories
enclosed by singing.

Sometimes the animals dream of evil
in the form of soap and metal
but mostly the animals dream
of other animals.

There are exceptions:

> the silver fox in the roadside zoo
> dreams of digging out
> and of baby foxes, their necks bitten
>
> the caged armadillo
> near the train
> station, which runs
> all day in figure eights
> its piglet feet pattering,
> no longer dreams
> but is insane when waking;
>
> the iguana
> in the petshop window on St. Catherine Street
> crested, royal-eyed, ruling
> its kingdom of water-dish and sawdust
>
> dreams of sawdust.

## AT THE TOURIST CENTER IN BOSTON

There is my country under glass,
a white relief-
map with red dots for the cities,
reduced to the size of a wall

and beside it 10 blownup snapshots
one for each province,
in purple-browns and odd reds,
the green of the trees dulled;
all blues however
of an assertive purity.

Mountains and lakes and more lakes
(though Quebec is a restaurant and Ontario the empty
interior of the Parliament Buildings),
with nobody climbing the trails and hauling out
the fish and splashing in the water

but arrangements of grinning tourists—
look here, Saskatchewan
is a flat lake, some convenient rocks
where two children pose with a father
and the mother is cooking something
in immaculate slacks by a smokeless fire,
her teeth white as a detergent.

Whose dream is this, I would like to know;
is this a manufactured
hallucination, a cynical fiction, a lure
for export only?

I seem to remember people,
at least in the cities, also slush,
machines and assorted garbage. Perhaps
that was my private mirage

which will just evaporate
when I go back. Or the citizens will be gone;
run off to the peculiarly—
green forests
to wait among the brownish mountains
for the platoons of tourists
and plan their odd red massacres.

Unsuspecting
window lady: I ask you:

Do you see nothing
watching you from under the water?

Was the sky ever that blue?

Who really lives there?

## BACKDROP ADDRESSES COWBOY

Starspangled cowboy
sauntering out of the almost-
silly West, on your face
a porcelain grin,
tugging a papier-mâché cactus
on wheels behind you with a string,

you are innocent as a bathtub
full of bullets.

Your righteous eyes, your laconic
trigger-fingers
people the streets with villains:
as you move, the air in front of you
blossoms with targets

and you leave behind you a heroic
trail of desolation:
beer bottles
slaughtered by the side
of the road, bird
skulls bleaching in the sunset.

I ought to be watching
from behind a cliff or a cardboard storefront
when the shooting starts, hands clasped
in admiration,

but I am elsewhere.

Then what about me

what about the I
confronting you on that border
you are always trying to cross?

I am the horizon
you ride towards, the thing you can never lasso

I am also what surrounds you:
my brain
scattered with your
tincans, bones, empty shells,
the litter of your invasions.

I am the space you desecrate
as you pass through.

---

# *Earle Birney*

## THE BEAR ON THE DELHI ROAD

Unreal   tall as a myth
by the road the Himalayan bear
is beating the brilliant air
with his crooked arms
About him two men   bare
spindly as locusts   leap

One pulls on a ring
in the great soft nose    His mate
flicks    flicks with a stick
up at the rolling eyes

They have not led him here
down from the fabulous hills
to this bald alien plain
and the clamorous world    to kill
but simply to teach him to dance

They are peaceful both    these spare
men of Kashmir    and the bear
alive is their living    too
If    far away on the Delhi way
around him galvanic they dance
it is merely to wear    wear
from his shaggy body the tranced
wish forever to stay
only an ambling bear
four-footed in berries

It is no more joyous for them
in this hot dust to prance
out of reach of the praying claws
sharpened to paw for ants
in the shadows of deodars
It is not easy to free
myth from reality
or rear this fellow up
to lurch    lurch with them
in the tranced dancing of men

*Srinagar 1958—Île des Porquerolles 1959*

## TWENTY-THIRD FLIGHT

Lo as I pause in the alien vale of the airport
fearing ahead the official ambush
a voice languorous and strange as these winds of Oahu
calleth my name and I turn to be quoited in orchids
and amazed with a kiss perfumed and soft as the lei
Straight from a travel poster thou steppest
thy arms like mangoes for smoothness
o implausible shepherdess for this one aging sheep
and leadest me through the righteous paths of the Customs
in a midst of my own wild hopes
Yea though I walk through the valley of Immigration
I fear no evil    for thou art a vision beside me
and my name is correctly spelled
and I shall dwell in the Hawaiian Village Hotel
where thy kindred prepareth a table before me
Thou restorest my baggage    and by limousine leadest me
to where I may lie on coral sands by a stream-lined pool

Nay but thou stayest not?
Thou anointest not my naked head with oil?
O shepherdess of Flight Number Twenty-three only
thou hastenest away on thy long brown legs to enchant
thy fellow-members in Local Five of the Greeters' Union
or that favored professor of Commerce mayhap
who leadeth thee into higher courses in Hotel Management
O nubile goddess of the Kaiser Training Programme
is it possible that tonight my cup runneth not over
and that I shall sit in the still pastures of the lobby
whilst thou leadest another old ram in garlands past me
and    bland as papaya    appearest not to remember me?
And that I shall lie by the waters of Waikiki    and want?

*Honolulu 1958*

## MEETING OF STRANGERS

"Nice jacket you got dere, man"

He swerved his bicycle toward my curb
to call    then flashed round the corner
a blur in the dusk    of somebody big
redshirted    young    dark    unsmiling

As I stood hoping for a taxi to show
I thought him droll at least
A passing pleasantry?    It was frayed
a sixdollar coat    tropical weight
in this heat only something with pockets
to carry things in

Now all four streets were empty
Dockland    everything shut

It was a sound no bigger than a breath
that made me wheel

He was ten feet away    redshirt
The cycle leant by a post farther off
where an alley came in    What?!

My turning froze him
in the middle of some elaborate stealth
He looked almost comic    splayed
but there was a glitter
under the downheld hand
and something smoked from his eyes

By God if I was going to be stabbed
for my wallet (adrenalin suffused me)
it would have to be done in plain sight
I made a flying leap
to the middle of the crossing
White man    tourist    surrogate    yes
but not guilty enough
to be skewered in the guts for it
without raising all Trinidad first
with shouts    fists    feet    whatever
— I squared round to meet him
and there was a beautiful taxi
lumbering in from a sidestreet
empty!

As I rolled away    safe as Elijah
Lucky as Ganymede
there on the curb I'd leaped from
stood that damned cyclist solemnly
shouting

"What did he say?" I asked the driver
He shrugged at the windshield
"Man dat a crazy boogoo
He soun like he say
'dat a nice jump you got too' "

*Port-of-Spain 1962*

## CANADA: CASE HISTORY

This is the case of a highschool land
deadset in adolescence
loud treble laughs and sudden fists
bright cheeks    the gangling presence
This boy is oriented well to sports
and the doctors say he's healthy
he's taken to church on Sunday still
and keeps his prurience stealthy
Doesn't like books (except about bears)
collects new coins    old slogans    jets
and never refuses a dare
His Uncle spoils him with candy of course
but shouts him down when he talks at table
You'll note he has some of his French mother's looks
though he's not so witty and no more stable
He's really much more like his Father and yet
if you say so he'll pull a great face
He wants to be different from everyone else
and daydreams of winning the global race
Parents unmarried and living apart
relatives keen to bag the estate
schizophrenia not excluded—
will he learn to grow up before it's too late?

*Ottawa 1945*

## THE MAMMOTH CORRIDORS

*From Vancouver, Canada's Pacific metropolis, the*
*tourist may drive east over the smooth Trans-Canada*
*Hiway through a*

Turning from the great islands drowning
in the morning's waves from Asia
my car heads me from the city's April
  cherry petals on the slick streets
  against the gutted mountains the billboards
  conjuring perfection    Tahiti
  orgasms of peace    death insurance

*thousand miles of towering Rockies to the prairies.*
*Crossing from the north shore at the spectacular*
*Lion's Gate, the motorist begins to trace in reverse*

Over the taut bridge    through the lonely park
my wheels will themselves to the shrieking

*the spectacular route taken by the first explorers*
*and hardy traders. Stanley Park, with its convenient*
*thruway, aquarium, totem poles (exact replicas of*
*originals now stored for preservation) . . . a thousand*
*acres of playground where Indians once camped . . .*

around the highrisers    the sullen leisured
dogs    and the rolling realtors
At Georgia and Howe my eye is caught
and dropped by Mrs. Crombie in a convertible
(my analyst's ex-)    Then the spastic traffic
of buyers and bought    pedlars of weed and soap
of acid and snow    of work and wonder
'as the world asketh'    in Skidrow's lanes

*Blessed with relaxing airs, Canada's third*
*largest city offers . . . yacht basins, beaches,*

*... panoramic view, where a modest cairn commemorates ... British Navy in 1729 ... possession of the North Pacific coast from the Spaniards who first came to trade with the natives ...*

Eastward an hour and the master I own
has rushed me to winter and wildness
and merely the gray road coiling and diminishing
upward like a dragon's tail swinges me off
from the unsupportable Real
  the tortured peaks
  only a breath more broken
  the blind dive of the canyons
  a scratch of a century deeper
  since those first compulsive whites
  the Searchers
  for gold  absolution  furs  Asia
  for a name  death  or mere difference
came hurtling in improbable canoes
  heavy with liquor and fear
  bearing their beads and syphilis
  muzzleloaders and god

*According to recent scientific theories, this was the route taken by the earliest Indians, at the end of the last Ice Age.*

but from the truths that compel me
up the land's one nerve like a virus
to undo in a single day my father's lifetime
of westering
  from my own lusts and neckties and novels
  from ulcers  vitamins  bulletins  *accidia*
i lie unshielded under each motel's roof

*Convenient to transcontinental railroads and a four-lane hiway ... offers American visitors every modern ... angler's paradise  big game ...*

under the uncontrollable cliffs and the starlight
falling on the same ice-bitten ranges
the first men saw

*Having crossed from Asia to Alaska, and followed the mammoths down corridors in the melting ice-cap, these earliest Canadians are thought to have reached a dead-end in their progress south, and been forced to turn west from the Albertan plains into the Rockies and so eventually came to the Pacific.*

in that century the Siberians took  or more
(and took a hundred centuries ago)
to move by floes and hunger past the point
of no return  trailing the great woolly ones
  watching for the gleam of nine-foot tusks
  tracking  floundering  in the newborn earth
  wolving by the black rivers that rattled
  from the glare of the narrowing icewalls
till the last red fountains
(*Mammuthus parelephas columbi*  his blood)
gushed on the boggy tundra
at the blind corridor's end

*In the nearby museum, mounted specimens of the wild life,*

Surviving westward then over howling summits
to possess these still fresh-hewn alps
(which i inheriting do not possess)
  moving by day through bear and elk
  and by their killing
outliving sleep by capturing the deer's Wit
the Power of cougar
  in nets of dance and word
  the medicine of mask
  the threat of drum

*and a spacious diorama outlining the story of*
*man. No charge.*

Three mornings now from the applefoam
and the seas my Engine unreels me
out from the last gouged hills
like a bull straightens
into the prairie's arena
charges in a dazzle of snow the human mesh

*Through Calgary, where the Blackfoot trail*
*once crossed, a four-lane artery helps speed*
*the traffic of Canada's greatest car-per-capita*
*city . . . in Bowness Park, life-sized models of*
*dinosaurs that once roamed the area*

where all began for me
though the log cabin where first i was forced
into air
is a lost ghost under a vanished bridge
by a dying river

*In 1912 Stampede Day was inaugurated to perpetuate*
*the finest traditions of the pioneer and cowpuncher . . .*
*now a week of parades, racing, rodeos, and other*

An ash of ice whines at the crosses of streets
A morning drunk is spattering curses
over a halfbreed girl in a blotched doorway

*picturesque events . . . for the traveller from*
*the west, Calgary is the beginning of the*
*great Canadian prairie, which though largely*
*treeless, contains some of the world's richest*
*wheat-farms and oil deposits . . .*

Eastward again i am pulled to the sky
of land flattened white to the Pole
drawn against the unstillable winds
  the breath of that madcap virgin
  mother of ice
  who embraced it all
  a wink ago in the world's eye
  till the sun won us again
  with his roving glance
  and sent her shrinking and weeping
  frozen lakes over the upstart grass

*To the north, however, the rich postglacial soil eventually gives place to tundra, permafrost and Arctic conditions . . .*

Hoarding her cold passion she lies
the Greenland lodger
and the land's long face    and mine
cannot forget    is graved
with her monstrous rutting
Her time is our secret clock
She waits for all to slow
Then to lust back
wider than Europe and Pacific deep
  bringing her love    the rounded silence
  a long hard peace

Note: For the italicized quotations, acknowledgments are gratefully made to Alfred Stettler's *Guide to the Canadian West* (Midnapore, Alberta; Prairie Flower Press, 1964.)

# *bill bissett*

## NUCLEAR CIRCULAR

living now
in terribul
times

a circular came this morning
for which i had not askd
tho i now do ask
for th morning to come

prepared by th Government
telling me
that th advantages
of staying to leaving
—evacuating— Vancouver
cancel each other out

as we peopul cancel
out ourselves/th bomb up there
symbol of our hesitancies

reason — we sum of us saw thru that
so that now everyone decides

love — we now sum of us see thru
to hold our own land
put up barricades
when bad ones attack
without prediction
for they always change as our minds now do

th circular sd not to forget
to turn off th lights and gas
when leaving
and to have sum responsible member
of th family make certain there is enough
fuel for th family car
shud yu decide to leave
tho to leave is not obligatory

to leave is not obligatory

we do not have a family car or fuel
or provisions or friends in th country
who cud put us up until fallout goes

my friend sz to drink beer
be drunk for th hearty bomb,
laugh, i've taken stronger
forgetmenots than beer

can my precious little love
for i like most have turnd away

more than i held to, allowd

reach those peopul
who printed this circular
which robs me of my peace
which carries me to those few
i have with me i love
to this typewriter/breaking
                    down on me

POEM

when th littul man
came out of th sewing machine

we naturally stood
in what became a circle
around

this ordinary
wonder

thing was
what he told us was
what its like
to live in a sewing machine

th man in the moon
only tells us what its like
to live there: we might
only want to visit

last time we phondup God
to ask what shall we do
He sd well its a warm night
up here
whats it like down there

O cumon God you know
very well what its Like down
here

No i really dont god sd
well we certainly hung up (on him)
i dont think weve phond him since
in fact i think they had the line removd

# *George Bowering*

## ESTA MUY CALIENTE

On the highway
near San Juan del Rio
we had to stop the car
for a funeral.

The whole town it was
a hundred people or
two hundred
walking slowly along the highway

toward the yellow domed church
on the top of the hill
and we pulled into the shade
of a shaggy tree.

I turned off the engine
and we heard their music
a screeching saxophone
and high broken noted trumpet

alone and sad in the hot afternoon
as they walked slow like sheep
the women with black shawls
the men in flappy trousers.

Every five minutes the men
threw cherry bombs into the air
behind them: loud gun shots
blasting the afternoon

then the saxophone: tin music
odd tortured jazz
in that mysterious Indian Christian march
up the hill: bearing a coffin to the priest.

It was a small coffin
on the shoulder of one man in front
        the father we thought
the cherry bombs were like violence

against us: but we were stopped.
An old rattling truck
nosed thru them: and they closed
together again behind it
                                    ignoring us.

I walked away from the road
in among the bushes and prickly pear
looking for scorpions on the hot sand
and took a leak beside a thin horse.

An hour later the road was clear
and as I got in the car
a man on a donkey came by
a San Juan lonely in the mountains man.

Good afternoon, I said.
Good afternoon, he said, it is very hot.
Yes it is, I said, especially for us.
It is very hot for us too, he said.

## THE CANADA COUNCIL POET

ran into me yesterday
in a second-hand book store

& again this morning
in a liquor store.

You're a true poet
he said from his line-up.

I mentioned that I
hadn't seen him last week

in the police station.

---

# *Jim Brown*

## PORTRAIT

Your teeth are crooked
        You have amazing eyes

one day in the wind
        we climbed down the cliff
and ran by the sea

Your hair won't go up right
        when you hurry,
the composition won't write itself,
        things overwhelm you

You have two smiles
        one for the world
and one when you forget

once when I kissed you
        I felt an ocean flow
through us

You startle the air
when you speak
Your hair won't go up
You have amazing eyes.

---

# *Ivan Burgess*

## AS HE LAY DYING

I stood close by
In solemn silence
Respectful silence
Expected silence
As life ebbed
Slowly ebbed
Cruelly ebbed
Away from his being.

My mother was there
My father was there
My sister was there
My uncle was there
Two aunts were there
A cousin was there

And HE was there
In bed
Stretched out
Dying
Slowly dying
The pivot of our silence.

And we were all there
And saw death
Claim its umpteenth victim
As life ceased
And agony with it
And worry too.

Then voices rose
Like a sprung mouse trap;
Voices that shattered
That solemn, respectful, expected
Silence.

---

# *Leonard Cohen*

## FOR E.P.J.

I once believed a single line
    in a Chinese poem could change
        forever how blossoms fell
and that the moon itself climbed on
    the grief of concise weeping men
        to journey over cups of wine
I thought invasions were begun for crows
    to pick at a skeleton
        dynasties sown and spent
to serve the language of a fine lament
    I thought governors ended their lives
        as sweetly as drunken monks
telling time by rain and candles
    instructed by an insect's pilgrimage
        across the page—all this
so one might send an exile's perfect letter
to an ancient hometown friend

I chose a lonely country
      broke from love
            scorned the fraternity of war
I polished my tongue against the pumice moon
      floated my soul in cherry wine
            a perfumed barge for Lords of Memory
to languish on to drink to whisper out
      their store of strength
            as if beyond the mist along the shore
their girls their power still obeyed
      like clocks wound for a thousand years
I waited until my tongue was sore

Brown petals wind like fire around my poems
      I aimed them at the stars but
            like rainbows they were bent
before they sawed the world in half
      Who can trace the canyoned paths
            cattle have carved out of time
wandering from meadowlands to feasts
      Layer after layer of autumn leaves
            are swept away
Something forgets us perfectly

# *John Robert Colombo & William Lyon Mackenzie*

## THE FRENCH IN QUEBEC

As to the friendship of the Canadians of French origin
towards the English, Scotch and Irish—
perhaps it is less warm than I had supposed—
but, be this as it may,
it is us who are to blame.
England conquered their country—
turned their *colleges into a barrack*—
kept their people in ignorance—
insulted their leading men—
neglected their best interests—
forgot to conciliate and trust in them—
preferred strangers to their language, manners and customs—
*appeared* to give them popular institutions forty years ago
and now declares them virtually unfit to enjoy them!
The executive council contemplated in 1791,
did not turn the governor into a mere machine
to execute orders from London,
and his council into *dummies* set up for a show.

## *Frank Davey*

### THE FACT

Dark bars keep moving
over the naked moon.

You sit relaxed
                    beside me
small hand shifting the gears,
while I
        drive quickly thru the slatted night
humming

---

## *Kildare Dobbs*

### SONG FOR CONFORMISTS

Let's not do anything different honey,
Let's not try anything new—
Sex and all that
Is kind of old hat;
Love as a word
Is slightly absurd—
But what is there left to do?

    It's no use shocking the bourgeois,
    It's no use climbing the wall;
    No use shooting the pianist—
    He's doing his best, after all.
    It's no use raging and fighting
    To keep our difference warm—
    So let's do our best to keep in with the rest
    And conform, conform, conform.

Let's buy a house in the suburbs,
Let's go south when it's cold.
Let's be mature and adjusted—
But let's not ever grow old.
Let's get a job that's rewarding
—With a *challenge*!
                    —that isn't too hard!
Let's keep up with the Joneses
And stay in our own backyard.

Let's not do anything different honey,
Let's not try anything new—
Sex may be stale
As old ginger ale;
Love in a way
Is sort of *passé*—
But what is there left to do?

It's no use shooting your mouth off,
It's no use waking the zoo.
No use gunning the motor
Or telling the cops what to do.
Family life is outmoded
—But any port in a storm!
Let's not be too proud to follow the crowd
And conform, conform, conform.

---

# *Louis Dudek*

## INSCRIPTIONS

I have read inscriptions on the walls of public places,
the folk-art of the people,
and the News for which the crowd stood in the rain waiting . . .

And I thought of that girl and her boy in ancient Pompeii
who scribbled on a wall,
"I love you," and "We made love here,"

and of that captain of hosts in Sinai
leaving the silver mines, who wrote on a wall
"I was here,
I was in charge of the business."

---

# *R. G. Everson*

## WHEN I'M GOING WELL

When I'm going well
as now at Westmount Glen and CPR
in wet October dusk, the winds
taste firecrackery. Loud sparks
jump up laughing like a Breughel bride.
Crayoned in phosphorus, the station agent
vibrates. He's electrocuted.

When I'm electrocuted
weather doesn't matter:   wet
dusk of October flashes fire well
like Summer moon, March mud.
I dance on tiptoe mind along the platform
shaking laughter's outstretched hands
that shock me like a Winter lightswitch.

When I'm a Winter lightswitch
I pick allusions off the railway tracks.
Climbing a signal standard, I wave my hat.
A girl walking by along the platform
explodes the whole Glen area.

# *Doug Fetherling*

## NIGHT BEFORE LAST

sixty eight mph
four in car
howling
county road
two am
dollar a bottle
new york port
thick smoke
second floor party
everyone took off
his clothes
someone cowered
in corner
bongos and harmonica
playing
returning
speeding
highway brownshirt
bad time
to appear in court
finally
close to dawn
piled out
slept on couch
late sunday
dreamt of sandburg

## *Robert Finch*

### CAMPERS

THINK of each house you stay in as a tent
That holds you insecure from wear and tear,
And do not let its neighbourhood grow dear,
And never call its welcome permanent.

Others have loved such rooms and made them gay
Only to see them vanish from their sight
Leaving them on a vacant lot at night
Without a refuge from the threatening day.

Each fire you sit by is a fire in camp
Built of the driftwood from a transient shore,
And in remoter harbours will be more,
And other windows for the ousted lamp.

Cut yourself clear from growing to a wall
Since either you must leave or it must fall.

---

## *Len Gasparini*

### COLD-WATER FLAT BLUES

I can't even afford an old car!
& since I recently abandoned the idea
of spending the rest of my wretched nights
sleeping in Laundromats & subways—
I rented a cold-water flat. Not bad
for a start, eh? At least I'll be able
to endure my poverty in private.

Now everything's OK — except for my
landlord . . . a parsimonious old bastard
if ever there was one . . . afflicted
with pleurisy & voyeurism

I can't even afford an escritoire!
& a perpetual writer's cramp prevents
me from using toilet tissue properly.
Ugh! What a mess I'm in!
The urine-yellow wallpaper was peeling,
so I covered the scabs with colorful maps
cut out of a stolen atlas.

Now I'm subsisting on sardines, apples
& peanut butter sandwiches. If I can't
live like a king I'll certainly
eat like one. But I'm fed up!

I was born under a cold blue star!
& my only weapons are a zip gun that shoots
poems, a shiv that stabs aesthetically, &
brass knuckles that strike with metaphoric
force. Now I'll go out & rob a public
library & kidnap a few editors — or something.
How else can an honest poet earn a living?

---

# *Eldon Grier*

## TONY AT SEA

Tony has his work cut out
with his pretty new wife,
she seems to be always
threatening the blues.

The first time I saw him perform
was at dinner when
alert as a dog he set out
to reverse her natural bent.

It was great. Everyone
became involved, the young
waiter from Liverpool, the head steward,
his father-in-law. Just the sight of him
seemed to make people uneasy.

He imitated me, and his old
college professor. He took off
rather too loudly for comfort
a dozen types of Englishmen.

Like an old vaudevillian
he ate through an inventory of the
ship's food, and when she was past giggling,
produced a seedy birthday cake.

That did it. With a whoop not unlike a
bloodthirsty hound he burst triumphantly in upon
the still little stalactites
of her sadness.

## BURY ME IN MY CADILLAC

Perfectly grooved
with God, of course,
as my quarterback,
I've breached the hillside of success,
the solidly tricked suburbia;
raked the ceremonial leaves,
fringed my famished fancy
with a flower bed.
Vested in perma-stone,
I cannot now turn back.
Geronimo!

# *George Johnston*

## THE ROLL CALL

Names of my aunts in order: Mrs. Balls,
Mrs. McGonigle, Lou, old Great-aunt Hairy,
Gentle, unmentionable Aunt Beleek
Who's intricate in underwear and shoes,
Who's fickle in them, fiddled, fled, forgotten,—
My sweetest aunt, Beleek, and slightly rotten.

The roll call comforts me. Bless Aunt McGonigle,
Bless Mrs. Balls,
Bless all my aunts! I name their splendid names,
My queens of air, my dolls,
And my mortality, alas!

The day light passes. Night light passes too.
And all my aunts, however full in sight,
However giant-bowelled, breasted, sinewed,
Will founder, as the suns behind the chimneys;
Nor even fickle Aunt Beleek will linger,
Singled out by the somewhat smelly finger
Of recollection, poking among the drawers.
How can my wormy shelves and cupboards keep her
That have so many crumbling things to keep?

## WAR ON THE PERIPHERY

Around the battlements go by
Soldier men, against the sky—
Violent lovers, husbands, sons,
Guarding my peaceful life with guns.

My pleasures, how discreet they are:
A little booze, a little car,
Two little children and a wife
Living a small suburban life.

My little children eat my heart;
At seven o'clock we kiss and part,
At seven o'clock we meet again;
They eat my heart and grow to me.

I watch their tenderness with fear
While on the battlements I hear
The violent, obedient ones,
Guarding my family with guns.

---

# *George Jonas*

## PEACE

I wish to make a positive statement
Of happy hunters returning from the woods.
Wardens of dwindling flocks, serious concern
Dwells in their moist and beautiful eyes.

There is no conflict that love or bullets
Could not resolve in time.
Gardens are carefully planned . . . Long rows of roses sit
In all directions around any house.

There is always a period of peace
Between two blows, when a smiling landscape
Surrounds with blue light the resting warrior.
The raised arm hardly shows among the ferns.

At such times rabbits jump out of their trenches
And stand listening at the entrance of the field.
Worms pop out of the ground in open amazement,
Sharp-beaked birds freeze unfalling in their dive.

The moment is guarded by dustbins along the streets
Of low and crippled suburbs where later
Children come out of hiding and women pause for breath.
Hate, suspended, sways gently back and forth.

Rats are pacing the floor, thinking,
A loaf of bread cuts itself into warm slices,
A glass of milk travels to India,
Warships lean on their guns and close their eyes.

The beauty of such moments is hardly useful
Except for the purpose of missing a heartbeat,
As old men sit at tables, ready to talk.
For there is nothing to talk about.

# *Lionel Kearns*

## APPOINTMENT

The nightmare dog-pack
prowls
the suburb.

Yellow-eyed,
snarling,
they set their teeth
on parked cars
and lamp-posts,
and urinate
on the darkened
shopping-centre.

  Yards
  and sidewalks
  lie torn open
  by their ravening

  But they have not yet
  turned directly
  on the homes.

A black slit
opens
in the sky.
Look,

A little boy
is climbing
out of an abandoned
bus.

# *A. M. Klein*

## FRIGIDAIRE

EVEN in July it is our winter corner,
hill 70 of our kitchen, rising white
and cool to the eye, cool to the alpenfinger.
The shadows and wind of snowfall fall from its sides.

And when the door swings away, like a cloud blown,
the village is Laurentian, tiered and bright,
with thresholds of red, white roofs, and scattered greens;
and it has a sky and clouds, and a northern light.

Is peopled. On its vallied streets there stands
a bevy of milk, coifed like the sisters of snow;
and beaded bosoms of butter; and red farmhands;
all poised, as if to hear from the distant meadow,

there on the heights, with its little flowers of white,
the cubes that seem to sound like pasture bells.
Fixed to that far-off tinkle they don't quite
hear, they stand, frozen with eavesdropping, like icicles.

And there on the heights, the storm's electric, thriving
with muffled thunder, and lightning slow and white!
It is a private sky, a weather exclusive,
a slow, sensational, and secret sight.

## POLITICAL MEETING

FOR CAMILLIEN HOUDE

On the school platform, draping the folding seats,
they wait the chairman's praise and glass of water.
Upon the wall the agonized Y initials their faith.

Here all are laic; the skirted brothers have gone.
Still, their equivocal absence is felt, like a breeze
that gives curtains the sounds of surplices.

The hall is yellow with light, and jocular;
suddenly some one lets loose upon the air
the ritual bird which the crowd in snares of singing

catches and plucks, throat, wings, and little limbs.
Fall the feathers of sound, like *alouette's.*
The chairman, now is charming, full of asides and wit,

building his orators, and chipping off
the heckling gargoyles popping in the hall.
(Outside, in the dark, the street is body-tall,

flowered with faces intent on the scarecrow thing
that shouts to thousands the echoing
of their own wishes.) The Orator has risen!

Worshipped and loved, their favourite visitor,
a country uncle with sunflower seeds in his pockets,
full of wonderful moods, tricks, imitative talk,

he is their idol: like themselves, not handsome,
not snobbish, not of the *Grande Allée! Un homme!*
Intimate, informal, he makes bear's compliments

to the ladies; is gallant; and grins;
goes for the balloon, his opposition, with pins;
jokes also on himself, speaks of himself

in the third person, slings slang, and winks with folklore;
and knows now that he has them, kith and kin.
Calmly, therefore, he begins to speak of war,

praises the virtue of being *canadien*,
of being at peace, of faith, of family,
and suddenly his other voice: *Where are your sons?*

He is tearful, choking tears; but not he
would blame the clever English; in their place
he'd do the same; maybe.

Where *are* your sons?

The whole street wears one face,
shadowed and grim; and in the darkness rises
the body-odour of race.

---

# *Frederick E. Laight*

## DROUGHT

I have seen tall chimneys without smoke,
And I have seen blank windows without blinds,
And great dead wheels, and motors without minds,
And vacant doorways grinning at the joke.

I have seen loaded wagons creak and sway
Along the roads into the North and East,
Each dragged by some great-eyed and starving beast
To God knows where, but just away—away.

And I have heard the wind awake at nights
Like some poor mother left with empty hands,
Go whimpering in the silent stubble lands
And creeping through bare houses without lights.

These comforts only have I for my pain:
    The frantic laws of statesmen bowed with cares
    To feed me, and the slow, pathetic prayers
Of godly men that somehow it shall rain.

---

# *Archibald Lampman*

## MORNING ON THE LIEVRE

Far above us where a jay
Screams his matins to the day,
Capped with gold and amethyst,
Like a vapour from the forge
Of a giant somewhere hid,
Out of hearing of the clang
Of his hammer, skirts of mist
Slowly up the woody gorge
Lift and hang.

Softly as a cloud we go,
Sky above and sky below,
Down the river; and the dip
Of the paddles scarcely breaks,
With the little silvery drip
Of the water as it shakes
From the blades, the crystal deep
Of the silence of the morn,
Of the forest yet asleep;
And the river reaches borne
In the mirror, purple gray,
Sheer away
To the misty line of light,
Where the forest and the stream
In the shadow meet and plight,
Like a dream.

From amid a stretch of reeds,
Where the lazy river sucks
All the water as it bleeds
From a little curling creek,
And the muskrats peer and sneak
In around the sunken wrecks
Of a tree that swept the skies
Long ago,
On a sudden seven ducks
With a splashy rustle rise,
Stretching out their seven necks,
One before, and two behind,
And the others all arow,
And as steady as the wind
With a swivelling whistle go,
Through the purple shadow led,
Till we only hear their whir
In behind a rocky spur,
Just ahead.

---

# *Pat Lane*

## ELEPHANTS

The cracked cedar bunkhouse hangs
behind me like a grey pueblo
in the sundown, where I sit
to carve an elephant
from a hunk of brown soap
for the Indian boy who lives
in the village a mile back
in the bush.

Fred, the alcoholic truck-driver,
and the cat-skinner, sit beside
me with their eyes closed; all
of us waiting out the last hour
until we go back on the grade—

and I try to forget the forever
clankclankclank across the grade
pounding stones and earth to powder
for hours in the mosquito-darkness
of the endless, cold mountain night.

The elephant takes form—
my knife caresses smooth soap,
scaling off curls of brown
which the boy saves to take home
to his mother in the village.

Finished,
I hand the carving to him
and he looks at the image of the great
beast for a long time, then
sets it on dry cedar
and looks up at me . . .
What's an elephant?
he asks me,
so I tell him of the elephants
and their jungles; the story
of the elephant graveyard
which no-one has ever found
and how the silent
animals of the rain-forest
go away to die somewhere
in the limberlost of distances
and he smiles at me—

tells me of his father's
graveyard where his people have been
buried for years; so far back
no-one remembers when it started
and I ask him where the graveyard is
and he tells me it is gone
now, where no-one will ever find it,
buried under the grade of the new
highway.

---

# *George T. Lanigan*

## A THRENODY

"The Ahkoond of Swat is dead"—Press Dispatch

What, what, what,
What's the news from Swat?
    Sad news,
    Bad news,
Comes by the cable led
Through the Indian Ocean's bed,
Through the Persian Gulf, the Red
Sea and the Med-
Iterranean — he's dead;
The Ahkoond is dead!

For the Ahkoond I mourn
    Who wouldn't?
He strove to disregard the message stern,
    But he Ahkoondn't.

Dead, dead, dead;
    Sorrow, Swats!
Swats wha' hae wi' Ahkoond bled,
Swats whom he had often led
Onward to a gory bed,
    Or to victory,
    As the case might be.
    Sorrow, Swats!
Tears shed,
    Shed tears like water,
Your great Ahkoond is dead!
    That Swat's the matter!

Mourn, city of Swat!
Your great Ahkoond is not,
But lain 'mid worms to rot:
His mortal part alone, his soul was caught
(Because he was a good Ahkoond)
Up to the bosom of Mahound.
Though earthly walls his frame surround
(For ever hallowed be the ground!)
And sceptics mock the lowly mound
And say, "He's now of no Ahkound!"
(His soul is in the skies!)
The azure skies that bend above his loved
    Metropolis of Swat
He sees with larger, other eyes,
Athwart all earthly mysteries—
    He knows what's Swat.

Let Swat bury the great Ahkoond
With a noise of mourning and of lamentation!
Let Swat bury the great Ahkoond
With the noise of the mourning of the Swattish nation!
Fallen is at length
Its tower of strength,
Its sun had dimmed ere it had nooned:
Dead lies the great Ahkoond.
The great Ahkoond of Swat
is not.

---

## *Irving Layton*

### COMPOSITION IN LATE SPRING

When Love ensnares my mind unbidden
I am lost in the usual way
On a crowded street or avenue
Where I am lord of all the marquees,
And the traffic cop moving his lips
Like a poet composing
Whistles a discovery of sparrows
About my head.

My mind, full of goats and pirates
And simpler than a boy's,
I walk through a forest of white arms
That embrace me like window-shoppers;
Friends praise me like a Turkish delight
Or a new kind of suspender
And children love me
Like a story.

Conscience more flat than cardboard
Over the gap in a sole,
I avoid the fanatic whose subway
Collapsed in his brain;
There's a sinking, but the madonna
Who clings to my hairlock
Is saved: on shore the damned ones
Applaud with the vigour of bees.

The sparrows' golden plummeting
From fearful rooftop
Shows the flesh dying into sunshine.
Fled to the green suburbs, Death
Lies scared to death under a heap of bones.
Beauty buds from mire
And I, a singer in season, observe
Death is a name for beauty not in use.

## HOW POEMS GET WRITTEN

Like
a memory
torn
at the shoulders,
my darling
wears
the chemise
I gave her -
a wedding gift.

At night
I tap out
my poems
on her hip bone.

When
she can't
sleep
either
we write
the poem
together.

## THE SATYR

My Lovely, my impossible Love,
In a lane in Kishinev
Three hundred years ago
Silent in a quiet place
An old Greek with light green eyes
And wrinkled face
Sits and stares and sees nothing at all.

The years fall before him like a decayed wall.

And resurrected in the rooms
Of gambling houses
The violins scrape
And the Magyar women are beautiful
And the Magyar women have kissable napes
Perfumed and beautiful their blouses.

Quadrilles, mazurkas play everywhere
Play with a bold, intoxicating air
I could put on a caftan
A red fez, a turban
And sweep you into my arms
Across the roofs and churches of St. Catherine.

Ah, what bands! what crowds!

I tell you, my inviolate Love,
Till you and I embrace,
This Greek, trouserless and undignified,
Too old himself to sing or dance
His quiet gaze lost in the distance
Must like some ill-used god
Smoke his infernal pipe
And turn his green insensate eyes on us.

And you and I smoulder and burn.

## ON SEEING THE STATUETTES OF EZEKIEL AND JEREMIAH IN THE CHURCH OF NOTRE DAME

They have given you French names
        and made you captive, my rugged
troublesome compatriots;
        your splendid beards, here, are epicene,
plaster white,
        and your angers
unclothed with Palestinian hills quite lost
in this immense and ugly edifice.

You are bored—I see it—sultry prophets
        with priests and nuns
(What coarse jokes must pass between you!)
        and with those morbidly religious
i.e. my prize brother-in-law
                                ex-Lawrencian
pawing his rosary, and his wife
sick with many guilts.

Believe me I would gladly take you
    from this spidery church
its bad melodrama, its musty smell of candle
    and set you both free again
in no make-believe world
                    of sin and penitence
but the sunlit square opposite
alive at noon with arrogant men.

Yet cheer up Ezekiel and you Jeremiah
    who were once cast into a pit;
I shall not leave you here incensed, uneasy
    among alien Catholic saints
but shall bring you from time to time
                    my hot Hebrew heart
as passionate as your own, and stand
with you here awhile in aching confraternity.

## TO THE GIRLS OF MY GRADUATING CLASS

    Wanting for their young limbs praise,
Their thighs, hips, and saintly breasts,
    They grow from awkwardness to delight,
Their mouths made perfect with the air
    About them and the sweet rage in the blood,
    The delicate trouble in their veins.

    Intolerant as happiness, suddenly
They'll dart like bewildered birds;
    For there's no mercy in that bugler Time
That excites against their virginity
    The massed infantry of days, nor in the tendrils
    Greening on their enchanted battlements.

Golda, Fruma, Dinnie, Elinor,
My saintly wantons, passionate nuns;
O light-footed daughters, your unopened
Brittle beauty troubles an aging man
Who hobbles after you a little way
Fierce and ridiculous.

---

# *Dennis Lee*

## 400: COMING HOME

You are still on the highway and the great light of
moon comes over the asphalt, the gravelled
shoulders. You are on the highway, there is a kind of
laughter, the cars pound
south. Over your shoulder the scrub-grass, the fences,
the fields wait patiently as though someone
believed in them. The light has laid it
upon them. One
crow scrawks. The edges
take care of themselves, there is
no strain, you can almost hear it, you
inhabit it.

Back in the city many things you lived for are
coming apart. Transistor rock still fills
back yards, in the parks young men in consort do homage to
hondas, there will be
heat lightning, beer on the porches, goings on.
That is not it.

And you are still on the highway. There are no
houses, no farms. Across the median, past the swish and thud of
the northbound cars, beyond the opposite
fences, the fields, the
climbing highland, solitary in the
bright eye of the sun the
birches dance, and they
dance. They have
their reasons. You do not know
anything.
Cicadas call now, in the darkening swollen air there is dust
in your nostrils; a
kind of laughter; you are still on the highway.

## HE ASKS HER

What kind of
            pickle were we in? Every
    piddling triumph I dragged into the house—
                                        by the ears
            ("I fixed the washer in the outside tap.")
    by the snout
            ("I sold another book today. That makes eleven.")
    or by the curly Q of its little pink tale
            ("I seduced Madame Nhu this aft. In the john at
                                        Eglinton Station.")
                    —they all became weapons in the
                                        stockpile.
    Sometimes I trickled under the door to tell you
            sometimes I walked thru the wall, all shucks & left-
                                        handed
    sometimes I'd bound in via the second-storey window,
                hanging by my canine incisors.

But what kind of
pickle were we in? You had to
turn and finger the miserable little feat,
testing the cutting edge on your own flesh,
and I would savour the way something
closed inside me and fondled itself,
knowing that soon you'd be
cast down again, that I would be rejected.

---

# *Malcolm Lowry*

## CHRIST WALKS IN THIS INFERNAL DISTRICT TOO

Beneath the Malebolge lies Hastings Street,
The province of the pimp upon his beat,
Where each in his little world of drugs or crime
Moves helplessly or, hopeful, begs a dime
Wherewith to purchase half a pint of piss-
Although he will be cheated, even in this.
I hope, although I doubt it, God knows
This place where chancres blossom like the rose.
For on each face is such a hard despair
That nothing like a grief could enter there.
And on this scene from all excuse exempt
The mountains gaze in absolute contempt,
Yet this is also Canada, my friend,
Yours to absolve of ruin, or make an end.

## WITHOUT THE NIGHTED WYVERN

Notions of freedom are tied up with drink.
Our ideal life contains a tavern
Where man may sit and talk or just think,
All without fear of the nighted wyvern;
Or yet another tavern where it appears
There are no No Trust signs no No Credit
And, apart from the unlimited beers,
We sit unhackled drunk and mad to edit
Tracts of a really better land where man
May drink a finer, ah, an undistilled wine
That subtly intoxicates without pain,
Weaving the vision of the unassimilable inn
Where we may drink forever without owing
With the door open, and the wind blowing.

## OLD FREIGHTER IN AN OLD PORT

It had no name and we docked at midnight.
Nor could girls, shadowed at the dead car halt,
Laughing in linked quintets in the lamplight,
Leaven our hearts embittered with sea salt.
There was no beauty then about that place.
But waking early, to see near at hand
The wharf, road, and market, friendly clock face,
—The very lineaments of a new land—
Our flag run up the post office in spring,
Whose each stone seemed to promise news from one
Loved, and from our rusted bow the soaring
Car lines burning straight-ruled into the sun—
Emergence was of Christian from Despond
And Friday's print for Crusoe in the sand.

# *Pat Lowther*

## ON READING A POEM WRITTEN IN ADOLESCENCE

Couldn't write then maybe
but how I could love—
When I said "Tree"
my skin grew rough as bark.
I almost remembered how all the leaves
rushed shouting shimmering
out of my veins.

Even now
I can almost remember
how many hands I had
hooked in the sky.

---

# *L. A. Mackay*

## SNOW STORY

Suddenly light shone out from the dark window
and he moved more cautiously over the creaking snow.
Low boughs laid on his lips a cold finger
and sprang back, as the silence dropped, with a soft whir.
The shadow mink, by his moving step startled
skimmed like a thrown stone over the glitter. Cold
sucked at his muscles; powdery breath bit in his nostrils.
He listened at the clearing's edge. The house was still.

Deep in the cold dunes he swung north, in a cautious
drifting down, stealthily, on the blind side of the house.
Unheard he hid by the chimney, crept past the corner,
and laid stiff fingers on the capped latch of the door.
Suddenly thrust. The door swung; the snow tumbled
in from the banked drift, and the swift light spread
over the level swells, blank. The new-comer
stepped stiffly into the house; and the soft air
lapped at his eyelids. The last ember shivered,
flared in the cold gust, fell. Not a spark stirred.
He closed the door, stood for a heavy instant
listening in the soft dark, then with a grunt
squirmed out of his coat, and turned towards the dead embers.
There was a gliding rustle in the frosty firs
or so he thought. But already the sharp bramble
slipped snake-toothed from the earthy edge of the hearth-sill
had trapped his ankles; the hard searching root-tip
plunged in his heart, as the fresh leaves brushed his lip.

---

# *Alexander McLachlan & A. W. Purdy*

## THE DEATH OF THE OX

Dumb friend—your troubles are over,
mine begin again in the dark forest
where we toiled many years together:
of all my misfortunes your death's the worst.

I wanted to owe no man anything,
I wanted independence, wanted it far more
than other men want women or need God,
and now I expect to be poor.

There's fallow to plow, land to clear,
and ten acres to be logged out—
Without my friend how can I pay my debts?
How can my children eat?

My friend and work-mate of the deep wilderness,
lost in the red sea of Indian Summer,
among the monster maples almost like them,
a great dumb giant bathed in the amber sun.

On warm days when the children picked lilies
they'd laugh and wreath your horns with flowers,
and climb you as if they'd found a new mountain,
while I stood watching in a kind of pain of love.

You're gone now, and there will be no other
yoked with me for war against the trees
and tangled roots of elms and maples,
with never whip or goad,
in partnership:
then nodding home to drink at the same well together,
and sleep soon.
With half the world slaves, the rest their masters,
our road turned a different way.

# *Annette & Jim Murray*

## BENOIT

My name it is Benoit,
it is Benoit.
Oh, my name it is Benoit,
it is Benoit.
My name it is Benoit,
and my home is Canada,
et je suis content de ça—
Damn your eyes!

My name it is Benoit,
Jean Benoit.
My name it is Benoit,
oui c'est moi—
Please don't call me Ben-oyt,
'cause I'm not from Detroit:
est-ce que vous comprenez ça?
Damn your eyes!

I'm in love with Betty Jane, Betty Jane,
I'm in love with Betty Jane, Betty Jane,
and I think she feels the same
but she can't pronounce my name,
Mon Dieu, what a shame!
Damn her eyes!

I went to the college for many years,
and I learned how to be an engineer.
When success was very near,
they said, "No Frenchmen here!"
Do you think that this is fair?
Damn your eyes!

Mary Jones, she smiled at me,
smiled at me.
Mary Jones, she smiled at me.
smiled at me.
I said, "Je vous aime cherie."
Mais elle n'a pas compris:
"Please speak English, mon ami."
Damn her eyes!

Oh, I hope the time will come,
time will come,
yes, I hope the time will come,
time will come:
I will ask, "Do you love me?"
She will answer, "Oui, cheri."
But until that happy day,
Damn her eyes!
But until that happy day,
Damn her eyes!

---

# *John Newlove*

## THEN, IF I CEASE DESIRING

Then, if I cease desiring
you may sing a song
of how young I was.

You may praise famous moments,
all have them, of the churches
I broke into for wine,

not praise, the highways
I travelled drunkenly
in winter, the cars I stole.

You may allow me moments,
not monuments, I being
content. It is little,
but it is little enough.

## THE FLOWERS

FOR MY BROTHER

It is raining outside, rain
streaks down the window to my left,
cars sluice water in the gutters
in the night, the round
neon clock-containing sign
hanging outside beside my window
sways in the wind and buzzes.

The flowers sprout everywhere,
in pots and boxes, on lawns
and trees, in gardens and ditches
the flowers are growing; the wet
wind will nourish them, cut
some down but feed the rest.

The sign crackles
and swings on its bar,
iron bar; the cars go by
all the night. They cut
a momentary trail and mark,
disappearing, on the wet
black pavement. The cars go by,
the police in their cars
prowl restlessly
up and down the rainy avenue
looking for interlopers, anyone
afoot at night in the rain,
the blue and dangerous
gun-hipped cops.

The car came smashing
and wrecking his face, his head,
poor hit hurt head
bleeding on the roadway
and in the cool hospital
night in bandages
and glued-on tape.

His eyes, they said,
were soft and easy
years ago. Now
he wears them cleverly
like some secret
coupled badge,
twin and original, dark
ice eyes that watch and assess
slowly what they have
fixed
on; his head does not move.

In the hospitals
with antiseptic nurses
stripping him, knife-
fisted surgeons bending down,
they cut, irony,
to save his life; and he stayed
days and years filled
with tantalizing drugs, interminable
dreams, tangled in bandages and
shocks, suspicions, a nonchalant
profusion of hopes and cures
surrounded by the tears
of his rainy crazy peers.

Rain, wind and spring, all things
drove him crazy and grow
flowers, flowers
that dance in the rain,

the bulging flowers that grew
in his head, plants
of evil or of god, some
holy epileptic angel, bloated
inhuman flowers shining
their bright colours
insistently, turning
slowly in the wind
and spring, torturous
creaking growths, thick
cancerous things
in the rain, stems
like the barrels of rifles,
fat lead bullet roots
gripping the damp earth.

And the cars
pass up and down
the streets, disappearing
trails, the blue police
pass, coughing delicately
behind their leathery fists,
guns dangling
from their hips, eyes
watching. My flowery clock
buzzes and mutters,
typewriter taps
like the rain. I breathe
as harshly as the wind.

## A LETTER TO LARRY SEALEY, 1962.

November 15th.

Gone past Hope, through Hell's Gate and the China Bar,
around the rock dynamite slides, in
with the timorous driver going 45 in 60-zones,
he unable to eat, complaining about his new false teeth,
how they hurt him and cut his gums, me
having sold at last my typewriter
after having tried to give it away
unsuccessfully, books, letters, poems,
shirts, stories, lies, mirrors, shoes and my cowboy hat,
all given into the hands of friends
for use or for keeping, I have arrived
in Cache Creek, on the way
to Edmonton, spending my little money
on hotel beds, bread and beef,
necessary comforts before the lull,
stopping too soon, unable to sleep, think,
relax, waiting for morning and the movement
to begin again.

November 16th, 730am.

Awakened in rain by the rap of the soft-woollen-
sweater-breasted desk-girl, she
only a wooden door away from naked me,
I shower and shave, dress, descend the stairs
for coffee, all I dare buy, and the road,
sleeping-bag rolled under an arm,
observing how my sound
becomes more sensual, and thicker, on the road,
as the prospects diminish,
how the commas and hyphens abound.

And 900am.

After coffee, Sail Along Silv'ry Moon playing,
Billy Vaughn, quick rides through Kamloops, Chase,
Salmon Arm, Canoe, then short ones
past Sicamous and other unnamable towns
lazily until an ancient half-ton truck
took me to Revelstoke where the new highway
is, no more Big Bend and its rocks.
                                                            Five minutes after,
the first salesman's car, Calgary by eight
and a safe paid room in the Sally Ann.

November 17th.

Buying a pack for the clumsy bag,
zoomed to Edmonton, north, the Hostel, to beds,
to breakfast mush and supper, bummed cigarettes,
sitting dull-eyed day-long in the railway station.
Edmonton. November. Cold. Snow. I am sitting
on the edge of the bed, scribbling on paper towels,
afraid of the ostentation; broke, tired, happy.

## NOT MOVING

Waterfalls
in so dark
& the noise

very much

        the animals
        undoubtedly
        moving there
        & waiting

rocks
rolling down
the gravel
cuts
of the road

there
bears be
pack rats (curious
to see) snakes
lizards

deer moving
among
the trees
quietly

also
on the side
of the road
me

smoking
nervously
at midnight
100 miles
to go

& cold
& afraid
on the side of the road
the only animal

not moving
at all

# *Alden Nowlan*

## IN THE HAINESVILLE CEMETERY

Not all these stones
belong to death. Here and there
you read something
like

John Andrew Talbot, 1885-1955
Mary, his wife, 1887—

and on decoration day
Mary will come here
and put a jam jar of water and tulips
on her own grave.

The Talbots are people
who make the beds before breakfast
and set the breakfast table
every night before they go to bed.

## SATURDAY NIGHT

Every five minutes they turn,
with their tires like sirens,
tusking the dirt up on the creek road,
and drive back through town—

slowing down on Main Street, manoeuvring
between the farmers' cars, hooting
at girls on the pavements who reply
with little hen movements, laughing, waiting.

The boys sport leather jackets and levis,
but that's their underwear,
the car is their real clothing:
at Taylor's Corner they turn again,
their Hollywood mufflers
making sounds furious, derisive, vulgar—
like a bear growling and breaking wind,

and roar through Main Street again.

## LAMENT FOR JAMES TALBOT

LATE MEMBER OF THE LEGISLATIVE ASSEMBLY OF NEW BRUNSWICK, REPRESENTING CONNAUGHT COUNTY, 1920-1952.

Bible, britches and tobacco spittin',
Jimmie Talbot was a whistlin' kitten,
hardshell preacher, ruttin' buck,
text, hot liquor and a ton of luck.

He was Moses-sweet hell, he'd juggle curses,
tell dirty stories and palaver verses.
He'd holler loud as a turpentined toad,
then speak soft as a sinner on the glory road.

Bible, britches and tobacco spittin',
Jimmie Talbot was a whistlin' kitten,
hardshell preacher, ruttin buck,
text, hot liquor and a ton of luck.

Jimmie'd spout from a rotten stump,
eat parsnip pancakes and pinch a rump,
Kept Connaught County dog-bone dry,
and never begrudged a pint to a guy.

Bible, britches and tobacco spittin',
Jimmie Talbot was a whistlin' kitten,
hardshell preacher, ruttin' buck,
text, hot liquor and a ton of luck.

Jimmie bewitched the county seat
with Shakespeare, Deficits and surplus wheat,
and carried Hainseville with ninety loads
of gravel and two months work on the roads.

## THE GIFT

"My son sent it," she says. The man-shaped stone
stands in its broken wrappings on the table,
defying measurement: six inches tall,
perhaps, but monstrous too, a brutal bulk
sensed in its attitude. Too starkly human.
"Esquimaux carve them," she explains. Her son
wrote her from Resolute. She laughs. "He says
it's like walking into a geography.
He always dreamed too much." The soapstone man
says nothing, though it's not impossible
that he might speak, having decided to,
since he appears ruthlessly objective
enough to be the image of some god.
If so, the old and unambiguous
kind who had hooves and buttocks. She won't say
what she thinks of this gift, except such things
as one must say of gifts from sons. It's plain
this hard and intimately squalid thing
shocks her. I see its gradual ascension
into the attic to be kept, forgotten.

## NANCY

Nancy was the smoking tines,
   the distance strawstack's blaze at night
when from my window all the dark
   closed darker on that light.

Nancy was the cool beneath
   the bridge where we were forty thieves.
Cars went over, gravel came down
   Nancy was this; and please

show me what Nancy is, I said,
   that part that never can be me.
And Nancy naked was Nancy clothed
   in denser mystery.

## STREET CORNER IDLER

His tragedy is that he seems to wait—
idlers should swagger in and entertain!
the tramps in mother's kitchen always paid
mouth organ tunes and stories sad as plays.

They had unfaithful sons and cheating wives
and when they left us it was strangely pleasant
to think of them, full of our beans and bread,
turning beside the gate to thumb their noses.

## I KNEW THE SEASONS ERE I KNEW THE HOURS

I knew the seasons ere I knew the hours;
the Christmas cactus blossomed anytime
after December first and scarlet flowers
fell patiently, in patterns like the blood
from shallow wounds, in mother's russet parlour.

I was once six and so damned lonely
I called love Rover, he had two sad ears,
a black-white checkerboard of face, a nose
for venison, he stole my uncle blind,
was caught and shot and buried in the pasture.

For months I sprinkled daises over him,
sucking my grief like lemons. Stephanie
shredded the daisies when she punished me
for being born her brother and we wrestled,
crushing the grass like lovers, till our mother
whipt us apart. Eventually the flowers
were laid less for my grief than for that struggle.

## THE BULL MOOSE

Down from the purple mist of trees on the mountain,
lurching through forests of white spruce and cedar,
stumbling through tamarack swamps,
came the bull moose
to be stopped at last by a pole-fenced pasture.

Too tired to turn or, perhaps, aware
there was no place left to go, he stood with the cattle.
They, scenting the musk of death, seeing his great head
like the ritual mask of a blood god, moved to the other end
of the field, and waited.

The neighbours heard of it, and by afternoon
cars lined the road. The children teased him
with alder switches and he gazed at them
like an old, tolerant collie. The woman asked
if he could have escaped from a Fair.

The oldest man in the parish remembered seeing
a gelded moose yoked with an ox for plowing.
The young men snickered and tried to pour beer
down his throat, while their girl friends took their pictures.

And the bull moose let them stroke his tick-ravaged flanks,
let them pry open his jaws with bottles, let a giggling girl
plant a little purple cap
of thistles on his head.

When the wardens came, everyone agreed it was a shame
to shoot anything so shaggy and cuddlesome.
He looked like the kind of pet
women put to bed with their sons.

So they held their fire. But just as the sun dropped in the river
the bull moose gathered his strength
like a scaffolded king, straightened and lifted his horns
so that even the wardens backed away as they raised their rifles.
When he roared, people ran to their cars. All the young men
leaned on their automobile horns as he toppled.

## THE EXECUTION

On the night of the execution
a man at the door
mistook me for the coroner.
"Press", I said.

But he didn't understand. He led me
into the wrong room
where the sheriff greeted me:
"You're late, Padre".

"You're wrong", I told him. "I'm Press".
"Yes, of course, Reverend Press".
We went down a stairway.

"Ah, Mr. Ellis", said the Deputy.
"Press!" I shouted. But he shoved me
through a black curtain.
The lights were so bright
I couldn't see the faces
of the men sitting
opposite. But, thank God, I thought
they can see me!

"Look!" I cried. "Look at my face!
Doesn't anybody know me?"

Then a hood covered my head.
"Don't make it harder for us", the hangman whispered.

---

# *Derek Pethik*

## THE NU NOLLEJ

*"A Saskatchewan educationalist asserts that producing well-rounded personalities is even more important than learning the niceties of grammar."—news item.*

The Schoolman of course they all praised to the skies;
He was clearly the man for the task
Of bringing the best, whether thought or expressed,
To the earnest young people of Sask.
His learning was wide, and he pointed with pride
To the fact that his pupils were grounded
Not in cruel repression, but free self-expression,
Which of course made them very well rounded.

"What's the use of such fetters as capital letters,
Punctuation, or similar crimes?"
So the Schoolman would cry, and the class would reply
"They are quote out of tune with the times!"

"Other schools are such shams, with their tests and exams,
But we've got our brave Schoolman to bless;
He has kept our minds free of such fiddle-dee-dee,
—Or of anything else, we confess."

But at college embarked, where they had to be marked,
At exam time, just what was their rank?
To say it was zero might slander our hero,
So we'll call it a (well-rounded) blank.

But though this dull college disdained the Nu Nollej,
The Schoolman did not start to curse it. He
Merely dreamed of the hour it would be in his power
To make it a Progressiversity.

---

# *A. W. Purdy*

## OLD ALEX

"85 years old, that miserable alcoholic
old bastard is never gonna die" the man said
where he got bed and board. But he did.
I'll say this about Alex' immortality tho:
if they dig him up in a thousand years
and push a spigot into his belly why
his fierce cackle'll drive a nail in silence,
his laugh split cordwood and trees kow-tow
like green butlers, the staggering world
get drunk and all the ghouls go scared—

So you say: was I fond of him?
No—not exactly anyhow. Once
he told his sons and daughters to get out,
and then vomited on their memory. It'd be
like liking toadstools or a gun pointing at you—
He sat home three weeks drinking whiskey,
singing harsh songs and quoting verse and chapter
from the Bible: his mean and privileged piety
dying slowly: they rolled him onto a stretcher
like an old pig and prettied him with cosmetics,
sucked his blood out with a machine and
dumped him into the ground like garbage—

I don't mourn. Nobody does. Like mourning an ulcer.
Why commemorate disease in a poem then?
I don't know. But his hate was lovely,
given freely and without stint. His smallness
had the quality of making everyone else feel noble,
and thus fools. I search desperately
for good qualities and end up crawling
inside that decaying head and wattled throat
to scream obscenities like papal blessings,
knowing now and again I'm at least God—
Well, who remembers a small purple and yellow bruise long?
But when he was here he was a sunset!

## PERCY LAWSON

CONTRACT NEGOTIATOR—VANCOUVER UPHOLSTERER'S UNION

Sitting with Lawson in 1954
        sitting with Percy Lawson
ill at ease in the boss's panelled office
after work hours talking of nothing
talking of practically almost nothing
a lousy nickel raise that is
        haggling over a lousy nickel
and maybe besides the long and hourly
bearable toil of an almost lifetime
(East Indians: 35 years
        Canadians: 70—figures approximate)
Listen in again in the boss's panelled office
        listen to Lawson
listen to Percy Lawson
—thinking of girls in the cutting room
afraid of the union
        afraid for their jobs and
thinking of me—afraid of Watt or
not afraid
        only wanting to be liked
and knowing for sure I'm not

Thinking of Lawson
          up from the coal mines
on the island and gotten fat
since talking and haggling and
being afraid of practically nothing
but death and his wife and damn near
          everything but not
not bosses
not Watt
And what's the contract news from Watt who
if I said what I thought he was would
sue me for damn near everything
would sue me right now in a poem and
get a judgement for one lying lyric
          I can't write
          (I'll be damned if I write)
in praise of Watt
in praise of
          practically nothing
But I listen to Percy Lawson
          haggling over a lousy nickel
listen to the sonuvabitch
          haggling over a lousy nickel
the twentieth part of a dollar that
          winks among the words
like a clean magician's coin
born from virginal nothing and not
mined or smelted and sweated and laboured for
the twentieth part of a wasted hour back there
in the silvery guts of a labouring terribly useful lifetime

In a tactical pause between the chop
          of words Lawson turns
the little fat man probably dead now
          turns then and gives
me a gold-toothed grin

## HOCKEY PLAYERS

What they worry about most is injuries
                    broken arms and legs and
fractured skulls opening so doctors
can see such bloody beautiful things
almost not quite happening in the bone rooms
                    as they happen outside—

And the referee?
                    He's right there on the ice
not out of sight among the roaring blue gods
of a game played for passionate businessmen
and a nation of television agnostics
who never agree with the referee and applaud
when he falls flat on his face—

                    On a breakaway
the centre man carrying the puck
his wings trailing a little
                    on both sides why
I've seen the aching glory of a resurrection
                    in their eyes
                    if they score
but crucifixion's agony to lose
—the game?

                    We sit up there in the blues
bored and sleepy and suddenly three men
break down the ice in roaring feverish speed and
we stand up in our seats with such a rapid pouring
of delight exploding out of self to join them why
theirs and our orgasm is the rocket stipend
for skating thru the smoky end boards out
of sight and climbing up the appalachian highlands

and racing breast to breast across laurentian barrens
over hudson's diamond bay and down the treeless tundra where
auroras are tubercular and awesome and
stopping isn't feasible or possible or lawful
but we have to and we have to
                                                    laugh because we must and
stop to look at self and one another but
                    our opponent's never geography
                                        or distance why
                         it's men
                         —just men?

And how do the players feel about it
this combination of ballet and murder?
For years a Canadian specific
to salve the anguish of inferiority
by being good at something the American's aren't—
And what's the essence of a game like this
which takes a ten year fragment of a man's life
replaced with love that lodges in his brain
                    and takes the place of reason?
Besides the fear of injuries
is it the difficulty of ever really overtaking
a hard black rubber disc?

Is it the impatient coach who insists on winning?
Sportswriters friendly but sometimes treacherous?
—And the worrying wives wanting you to quit and
your aching body stretched on the rubbing table
thinking of money in owners' pockets that might be in yours
the butt-slapping camaraderie and the self indulgence
of allowing yourself to be a hero and knowing
everything ends in a pot-belly—

Out on the ice can all these things be forgotten
in swift and skilled delight of speed?
—roaring out the endboards out the city
streets and high up where laconic winds
whisper litanies for a fevered hockey player—
Or racing breast to breast and never stopping
over rooftops of the world and all together
sing the song of winning all together
sing the song of money all together . . .

(and out in the suburbs
there's the six year old kid
whose reflexes were all wrong
who always fell down and hurt himself and cried
and never learned to skate
with his friends)—

## ABOUT BEING A MEMBER OF OUR ARMED FORCES

Remember the early days of the phony war
when men were zombies and women were CWACs
and they used wooden rifles on the firing range?
Well I was the sort of soldier you couldn't trust
with a wooden rifle
and when they gave me a wooden bayonet
life was fraught with peril for my brave comrades
including the sergeant-instructor
I wasn't exactly a soldier tho
only a humble airman
who kept getting demoted and demoted and demoted
to the point where I finally saluted civilians

And when they trustingly gave me a Sten gun
Vancouver should have trembled in its sleep
for after I fired a whole clip of bullets
at some wild ducks under Burrard Bridge
(on guard duty at midnight)
they didn't fly away for five minutes
trying to decide if there was any danger
Not that the war was funny
I took it and myself quite seriously
the way a squirrel in a treadmill does
too close to tears for tragedy
too far from the banana peel for laughter
and I didn't blame anyone for being there
that wars happened wasn't anybody's fault then
now I think it is

## INTERRUPTION

When the new house was built
callers came:
black squirrels on the roof every morning
between sleep and wakefulness,
and a voice saying "Hello dead man".
A chipmunk looks in the window
and I look out,
the small face and the large one
waver together in glass,
but neither moves
for the instant of our lifetimes.
Orioles, robins and red-winged blackbirds
are crayons that colour the air;
something sad and old
cries down in the swamp.

Moonlight in the living room,
a row of mice single file
route marching across the empty lunar plain
until they touch one of my thoughts
and jump back frightened,
but I don't wake up.
Pike in the lake pass and re-pass the windows
with clouds in their mouth.
For 20 minutes every night
the sun slaps a red paint brush
over dinner dishes and leftovers,
but we keep washing it off.
Birds can't take a shortcut home,
they have to go round the new house;
and cedars grow pale green candles
to light their way thru the dark.

Already the house is old:
a drowned chipmunk (the same one?)
in the rain barrel this morning,
dead robins in the roof overhang,
and the mice are terrified—
We have set traps,
and must always remember
to avoid them ourselves

## THE DRUNK TANK

A man keeps hammering at the door
(he is so noisy it makes my ears ache),
yelling monotonously, "Let me outa here!"
A caged light bulb floats on the ceiling,
where a dung-fly circles round and round;
and there is a greasy bolted-down steel bunk;
and a high barred window permitting
fungus darkness to creep in the room's corners.

The man keeps hammering at the door
until a guard comes:
"I just happen to know the mayor in this town,"
he tells the guard,
"and it's gonna be too bad for you
if you keep me locked up here."
The guard laughs and turns away.
"It's no use," I tell my cell mate.
"Just wait until morning,
then we'll be up in magistrate's court,
and being drunk isn't a very serious . . ."
"Who are you?" the man asks me.
"I don't know you."
"I'm your friend," I say to him,
"and I've been your friend a long time,
don't you remember?"
"I don't know you at all," he screams.
"Stay away from me!'
"If that's the way you feel about it," I say,
and suddenly I'm not so sure as I was,
memory is a funny thing isn't it?
"Please sit down and wait until morning,"
I say to him reasonably—
don't you think that was the right thing to say?
But he turns his back and hammers on the door:
"Guard! Guard! I want a cell by myself!
You've put a crazy man in here with me!"
He is so noisy.
And I watch him pounding on the black steel door,
a patch of sweat spreading on his back,
and his bald spot glistening—
He looks at me over his shoulder,
terrified,
and I spread my hands flat to show him
I have the best of intentions.
"Stay away from me Stay away!"

He backs off into a corner shaking,
while I sit down on the bunk
to wait for morning.
And I think:
this is my friend,
and I say to him,
"Aren't you my friend?"
But there he is at the door again,
he is so noisy . . .

---

# *James Reaney*

## KLAXON

ALL DAY cars mooed and shrieked,
Hollered and bellowed and wept
Upon the road.
They slid by with bits of fur attached,
Fox-tails and rabbit-legs,
The skulls and horns of deer,
Cars with yellow spectacles
Or motorcycle monocle.
Cars whose gold eyes burnt
With a too-rich battery,
Murderous cars and manslaughter cars,
Chariots from whose foreheads leapt
Silver women of ardent bosom.
Ownerless, passengerless, driverless,
They came to anyone
And with headlights full of tears
Begged for a master,
For someone to drive them
For the familiar chauffeur.

Limousines covered with pink slime
Of children's blood
Turned into the open fields
And fell over into ditches,
The wheels kicking helplessly.
Taxis begged trees to step inside,
Automobiles begged of posts
The whereabouts of their mother.
But no one wished to own them any more,
Everyone wished to walk.

---

# *Joe Rosenblatt*

## WAITER! . . . THERE'S AN ALLIGATOR IN MY COFFEE

Waiter! . . . there's an alligator in my coffee.
Are you trying to be funny?
he said:
what do you want for a dime . . . ?
. . . a circus?
but sir! I said,
he's swimming
around
and around
in my coffee
and he might
jump out on the table . . .
Feed him a lump of sugar! he snarled—
no! . . . make it two;
it'll weigh him down
and he'll drown.

I dropped two blocks of sugar
into the swamp,
two grist jaws snapped them up
and the critter—
he never drowned.
Waiter! . . . there's an alligator in my coffee.
Kill him! Kill him!
he said:
BASH HIS BRAINS OUT
WITH YOUR SPOON . . . !
By this time
considerable attention had been drawn:
around my coffee
the waiters, the owner,
and customers gathered.
What seems to be the trouble?
the owner inquired,
and I replied:
There's an alligator in my coffee!
. . . But the coffee's fresh, he said
and raised the cup to his nose . . .
Careful! I said,
he'll bite it
off
and he replied:
How absurd,
and lowered the cup
level to his mouth and
swallowed
the profit motive.

## THE WORK SHIFT

I gather my crooked work boots
that Christ should have worn
along the road to Golgotha
and the boots have a certain personality,
they're starved from a lack of polish and
broken through from labour, eaten by the very
life's dust, just like some people I know.
I place my warped feet inside the crooked boots.

Every afternoon (except Sat. and Sun.)
the round face of the "Silver Bell" alarm clock
laughs out a prolonged shrill dagger
that mutilates the egg shell world of my dream.
O how I love to sleep, I'm obsessed by sleep,
because I'm tired like those boots.
About 2:30 p.m. I'm out on the street, dragging
my clod-hoppers along the pavement and
I'm aware of the sparrows digging me over
with their J. Edgaring eyes:
at the corner of Avenue Road and Davenport,
the cops are loitering by the bank
like scarabs around a dung heap.

3:00 p.m. I'm at work unloading a C.P. Express trailer
and a wired box prison of miniature ground hogs
—guinea pigs marked up for the cancer factory—
moves along the belt:
so I think the only difference
between me and that family
is that I take a longer road to hell.

# *W. W. E. Ross*

## APOLOGIES TO ROBERT FROST

There wasn't any doubt of it at all.
Something was leaning up against the wall
That surely wasn't doing so before
I drove the yearling through the big barn door.
It might have been a rake, perhaps a hoe,
But what it was I really didn't know,
Though when I came to think of it I saw
My first impression must have had a flaw
And that it couldn't be a hoe or rake,
And so my first idea was a mistake.
"I'll go and see just what it is!" I said
But then I thought: "I'd better not be led
Into some act that's rash and liable
To bring me into trouble. I can tell
The story later with a happier end
If I am careful now and don't pretend
To knowing what I'm not supposed to know."
(Though, to make sure, I hadn't far to go.)
"I'll not try further looking for a thing
That may not want itself spied out. I'll bring
Trouble on myself and on it too
If I attempt to see the matter through.
When someone puzzles over things and searches
It's like being lost inside a clump of birches.
You try to find your way but only see
In front of you the white of every tree.
All look the same and it's no use to shout.
Not one will tell you how you can get out."

I thought it must have been the hired man
Taking a rest before his work began;
But after all I had no time to spare
To make quite certain what was leaning there.
My chores would occupy me all the day,
Or nearly, so I quickly turned away.
Of course, if it was just the hired man,
I could have spoken to him, with a plan
To question him, for he would not refuse
To answer me, by making some excuse.
(Though all in all, as I thought afterwards,
My questioning him might have led to words.)
At any rate I hope I make it clear
My going elsewhere wasn't out of fear.
The fact I went along another path
Spared me perhaps an unpleasant aftermath.
What difference did it make? A rake, a hoe,
The hired man? But that's the way things go.
And so I thought, "I'll let the matter rest
And spend the morning with a greater zest.
I'll walk around the pasture lot till noon.
When I come back I'm sure he will be gone,
And even if he hasn't gone away
I'll take another look another day."
There was more than one thing I had to do,—
And just one final word I'll leave to you;
Not very much, perhaps, but in my style,
And making the experience worth while.
Instead of looking closely when they see
Something that acts a little differently
People had better be content to stay
And wait till what's unusual goes away.

# *Duncan Campbell Scott*

## THE FORSAKEN

### I

ONCE in the winter
Out on a lake
In the heart of the north-land
Far from the Fort
And far from the hunters,
A Chippewa woman
With her sick baby,
Crouched in the last hours
Of a great storm.
Frozen and hungry
She fished through the ice
With a line of the twisted
Bark of the cedar,
And a rabbit-bone hook
All through the wild day,
Fished and caught nothing;
While the young chieftain
Tugged at her breasts,
Or slept in the lacings
Of the warm *tikanagan*.
All the lake-surface
Streamed with the hissing
Of millions of iceflakes
Hurled by the wind;
Behind her the round
Of a lonely island
Roared like a fire
With the voice of the storm
In the deeps of the cedars.

Valiant, unshaken,
She took of her own flesh,
Baited the fish-hook,
Drew in a grey-trout,
Drew in his fellows,
Heaped them beside her,
Dead in the snow.
Valiant, unshaken,
She faced the long distance,
Wolf-haunted and lonely,
Sure of her goal
And the life of her dear one:
Tramped for two days,
On the third in the morning,
Saw the strong bulk
Of the Fort by the river,
Saw the wood-smoke
Hang soft in the spruces,
Heard the keen yelp
Of the ravenous huskies
Fighting for whitefish:
Then she had rest.

## II

Years and years after,
When she was old and withered,
When her son was an old man
And his children filled with vigour,
They came in their northern tour on the verge of winter,
To an island in a lonely lake.
There one night they camped, and on the morrow
Gathered their kettles and birch-bark,
Their rabbit-skin robes and their mink-traps,
Launched their canoes and slunk away through the islands,
Left her alone forever,
Without a word of farewell,

Because she was old and useless,
Like a paddle broken and warped,
Or a pole that was splintered.
Then, without a sigh,
Valiant, unshaken,
She smoothed her dark locks under her kerchief,
Composed her shawl in state,
Then folded her hands ridged with sinews and corded with veins,
Folded them across her breasts spent with the nourishing of
 children,
Gazed at the sky past the tops of the cedars,
Saw two spangled nights arise out of the twilight,
Saw two days go by filled with the tranquil sunshine,
Saw, without pain, or dread, or even a moment of longing:
Then on the third great night there came thronging and
 thronging
Millions of snowflakes out of a windless cloud;
They covered her close with a beautiful crystal shroud,
Covered her deep and silent.
But in the frost of the dawn,
Up from the life below,
Rose a column of breath
Through a tiny cleft in the snow,
Fragile, delicately drawn,
Wavering with its own weakness,
In the wilderness a sign of the spirit,
Persisting still in the sight of the sun
Till day was done.
Then all the light was gathered up by the hand of God and
 hid in His breast
Then there was born a silence deeper than silence,
Then she had rest.

# *F. R. Scott*

## EXAMINER

The routine trickery of the examination
Baffles these hot and discouraged youths.
Driven by they know not what external pressure
They pour their hated self-analysis
Through the nib of confession, onto the accusatory page.

I, who have plotted their immediate downfall,
I am entrusted with the divine categories,
ABCD and the hell of E,
The parade of prize and the backdoor of pass.

In the tight silence
Standing by a green window
Watching the fertile earth graduate its sons
with more compassion—not commanding the shape
Of stem and stamen, bringing the trees to pass
By shift of sunlight and increase of rain,
For each seed the whole soil, for the inner life
The environment receptive and contributory—
I shudder at the narrow frames of our text-book schools
In which we plant our so various seedlings.

Each brick-walled barracks
Cut into numbered rooms, black-boarded,
Ties the venturing shoot to the master stick;
The screw-desk rows of lads and girls
subdued in the shade of an adult—
Their acid subsoil—
Shape the new to the old in the ashen garden.

Shall we open the whole skylight of thought
To those tiptoe minds, bring them our frontier worlds
And the boundless uplands of art for their field of growth?
Or shall we pass them the chosen poems with the foot-notes,
Ring the bell on their thoughts, period their play,
Make laws for averages and plans for means,
Print one history book for a whole province, and
Let ninety thousand read page 10 by Tuesday?

As I gather the inadequate paper evidence, I hear
Across the neat campus lawn
The professional mowers drone, clipping the inch-high green.

## LAURENTIAN SHIELD

Hidden in wonder and snow, or sudden with summer,
This land stares at the sun in a huge silence
Endlessly repeating something we cannot hear.
Inarticulate, arctic,
Not written on by history, empty as paper,
It leans away from the world with songs in its lakes
Older than love, and lost in the miles.

This waiting is wanting.
It will choose its language
When it has chosen its technic,
A tongue to shape the vowels of its productivity.

*A language of flesh and of roses.*

Now there are pre-words,
Cabin syllables,
Nouns of settlement
Slowly forming, with steel syntax,
The long sentence of its exploitation.

The first cry was the hunter, hungry for fur,
And the digger for gold, nomad, no-man, a particle;
Then the bold commands of monopoly, big with machines,
Carving its kingdoms out of the public wealth;
And now the drone of the plane, scouting the ice,
Fills all the emptiness with neighbourhood
And links our future over the vanished pole.

But a deeper note is sounding, heard in the mines,
The scattered camps and the mills, a language of life,
And what will be written in the full culture of occupation
Will come, presently, tomorrow.
From millions whose hands can turn this rock into children.

---

# *Robert Service*

## FIVE-PER-CENT

Because I have ten thousand pounds I sit upon my stern,
And leave my living tranquilly for other folks to earn.
For in some procreative way that isn't very clear,
Ten thousand pounds will breed, they say, five hundred
 every year.
So as I have a healthy hate of economic strife,
I mean to stand aloof from it the balance of my life.
And yet with sympathy I see the grimy son of toil,
And heartily congratulate the tiller of the soil.
I like the miner in the mine, the sailor on the sea,
Because up to five hundred pounds they sail and mine for me.
For me their toil is taxed unto that annual extent,
According to the holy shibboleth of Five-per-Cent.

So get ten thousand pounds, my friend, in any way you can,
And leave your future welfare to the noble Working Man.
He'll buy your suits of Harris tweed, an Airedale and a car;
Your golf clubs and your morning *Times*, your whiskey and cigar.
He'll cosily instal you in a cottage by a stream,
With every modern comfort, and a garden that's a dream.
Or if your tastes be urban, he'll provide you with a flat,
Secluded from the clamour of the proletariat.
With pictures, music, easy chairs, a table of good cheer,
A chap can manage nicely on five hundred pounds a year.
And though around you painful signs of industry you view,
Why should you work when you can make your money work
  for you?

So I'll get down upon my knees and bless the Working Man,
Who offers me a life of ease through all my mortal span;
Whose loins are lean to make me fat, who slaves to keep me free,
Who dies before his prime to let me round the century;
Whose wife and children toil in turn until their strength is spent,
That I may live in idleness upon my Five-per-Cent.
And if at times they curse me, why should I feel any blame?
For in my place I know that they would do the very same.
Aye, though they hoist a flag that's red on Sunday afternoon,
Just offer them ten thousand pounds and see them change
  their tune.
So I'll enjoy my dividends and live my life with zest,
And bless the mighty men who first—invented Interest.

# *A. J. M. Smith*

## THE LONELY LAND

Cedar and jagged fir
uplift sharp barbs
against the gray
and cloud-piled sky;
and in the bay
blown spume and windrift
and thin, bitter spray
snap
at the whirling sky;
and the pine trees
lean one way.

A wild duck calls
to her mate,
and the ragged
and passionate tones
stagger and fall,
and recover,
and stagger and fall,
on these stones—
are lost
in the lapping of water
on smooth, flat stones.

This is a beauty
of dissonance,
this resonance
of stony strand,
this smoky cry
curled over a black pine
like a broken

and wind-battered branch
when the wind
bends the tops of the pines
and curdles the sky
from the north.

This is the beauty
of strength
broken by strength
and still strong.

## TO HOLD IN A POEM

I would take words
As crisp and as white
As our snow; as our birds
Swift and sure in their flight;
As clear and as cold
As our ice; as strong as a jack pine;
As young as a trillium, and old
As Laurentia's long undulant line;

Sweet-smelling and bright
As new rain; as hard
And as smooth and as white
As a brook pebble cold and unmarred;

To hold in a poem of words
Like water in colourless glass
The spirit of mountains like birds,
Of forests as pointed as grass;

To hold in a verse as austere
As the spirit of prairie and river,
Lonely, unbuyable, dear,
The North, as a deed, and forever.

# *Raymond Souster*

## FLIGHT OF THE ROLLER-COASTER

Once more around should do it, the man confided . . .

and sure enough, when the roller-coaster reached the peak
of the giant curve above me, screech of its wheels
almost drowned out by the shriller cries of the riders,

instead of the dip and the plunge with its landslide of screams,
it rose in the air like a movieland magic carpet,
    some wonderful bird,

and without fuss or fanfare swooped slowly across
    the amusement-park,
over Spook's Castle, ice-cream booths, shooting-gallery.
    And losing no height

made the last yards above the beach, where the cucumber-cool
brakeman in the last seat saluted
a lady about to change from her bathing-suit.

Then, as many witnesses reported, headed leisurely
    out over the water,
disappearing all to soon behind a low-flying flight of clouds.

## THE VICTORY

It's a race to see which will reach
the cigarette butt first,
the hand reaching down into the gutter
or the snow-removal machine
gulping the slush for a long line of patient trucks.

Well, the hand wins
by a three-foot margin, and as the body
straightens up, prize in its shaky clutch,
there's that age-old, human smile
of victory!

## THE TOP HAT

Whether it's just a gag or the old geezer's
a bit queer in the head, it's still refreshing
to see someone walking up Bay Street
with toes out of shoes, patched trousers, frayed suit-coat,
and on his head the biggest, shiniest top hat
since Abe Lincoln,
                                        and walking as if the whole
damn street belonged to him:
                                                        which at this moment for my money
it does.

## THE INTRODUCTION

My first introduction to poetry:
our form master on the blackboard
breaking up one of the stanzas
from Wilfred Campbell's "August Reverie"
into principal and subordinate clauses.

## LAKE OF BAYS

"Well, I'm not chicken . . ."
that skinny ten-year old girl
balanced on the crazy-high railing
of the Dorset bridge:
                                        suddenly let go
down
fifty feet into the water.

"That one will never grow up
to be a lady," my mother said
as we walked away.

but I'll remember
her brown body dropping like a stone
long after I've forgotten
many many ladies . . .

## WHEN IT COMES MY TURN

When it comes my turn
to fall toward death, let me go
like the hollyhock over-reaching
his grab toward the sun, and heavy
from the height of it bending
crazily over, down
                                        to rest there
on the grass, calmly,
as if there were nothing else
worth straightening up for.

## THE BURIAL

After the censer's last swing
at the church door, hand released
from the casket's handle

the black hearse leads us
through the ten o'clock cool
summer sunshine up Keele Street
past the thousand deaths
of the slaughter-house animals
past the new suburbs out
into open country
timothy-cool, alfalfa-fresh
with brown barns, browner cows
sky a jeweller's blue
poet's dream
                        and feeling so alive
at the cemetery I wanted
to somehow wrench the top
off your coffin, girl so young to die,
and shine the sun down
on your white face to warm it
all the way from here
through the long way over
to eternity.

## THIS WIND

This wind comes charging at the house
like a creature unchained, puts its fists
through cracks around windows and gives
curtains enormous breasts, takes a bird
downwind and turns him every way, bruises
tree branches past endurance and leaves them wailing
after each onslaught, then goes careening
over the roof-tops, powdering the air
with snow-sugar.
O but this wind
of December is the same wind we'll later feel
soft as a girl's touch on our face, warmer
than her embrace, and coming with the scent
of just-opened lilacs sweeter than all
but her most mysterious, never-dreamt-of
long-past-midnight places!

## FREEZE UP

I wonder at
what exact moment
(I wish I'd been there)
something said "that's the very
last drop going over"

and the waterfall suddenly
couldn't budge and knew
it was so.

## SOMEONE HAS TO EAT

Someone has to eat
the two-day old bread,
cheap cans of peas
no one else wants,

so here on Queen East,
summer-heavy with flies,
coated over with dust,
ground under with heat,

this tired food waits
the ones who must finally
come here to buy

## SETTING THE TRAP

The man down the street near the corner
working near his front door
in the April dusk, holding
a can in his hand.
By the fresh hole
under his porch I can guess
what he's up to.
"The skunks are at it
early this year: we'll see
how they like a little lye."

He's a good man, really,
and if he were going to bed tonight
he'd sleep soundly. As it is,
when he comes here tomorrow morning
off the night shift, he'll curse
if there isn't at least one dead animal
to show for all his careful work.

# *Francis Sparshott*

## NEANDERTHAL NATIONAL ANTHEM

In the old Neander Valley, a happy missing link,
I was proud to be the putty in evolution's chink.
We had a family motto: it is earlier than you think
  In the old Neander Valley, my home.

When Grandpa Javanensis descended from the trees
His eyebrows met his hairline, his elbows knocked his knees.
That backward Asiatic lived far across the seas
  From the old Neander Valley, my home.

Sinanthropus at Pekin, Proconsul at the Cape
Had some approximation to a proper human shape,
But we would never speak to them—we're further from the ape
  In the old Neander Valley, my home.

When Dawson came to Piltdown and planted monkeys' jaws
He did it for the sake of the old Darwinian cause;
But I'm a proper fossil, and I grew by nature's laws
  In the old Neander Valley, my home.

In the old Neander Valley, the latest thing in man,
I lay around acquiring a deep all-over tan
Till along came homo sapiens and we all got up and ran
  From the old Neander Valley, my home.

# *Peter Stevens*

## WARMING UP, TUNING IN

A Cain-mark silver-livid burns
into my forehead;
its fierce needle-point disappears within
stitching itself inside my skull.
My flesh is bulging sloppy round my bone-case
as I stare at myself
set in the room curved round me
mirrored in the grey screen
until flickers of light blot me out
my gross body smashed
under the wide tracks of cars
then thrown ungainly mangled
in some small nameless village
where my children weep by the burning huts
huddling thin and frightened
by these grey phantoms from another world
carrying fire on their backs
jumping down from whirling spiders
to melt the living room.

The walls ooze like thick glue
slipping shapeless round me.
The glue turns my flesh to molten bubbles,
leaves only the chamber of my skull,
where a Buddhist priest sits
and calmly sets himself alight
burning with a silver-livid flame.

# *A. Szumigalski*

## VICTIM

Ah, the cliff edge, where so many murders are done!
Can't you see the body among the boulders
Far down on the beach?
White seagulls scream, they are filming
A frail girl in a thin nightgown
Prone on the distant rocks.

Mr. B. and I are walking hand in hand
Up the cliff path, knowing that
Under our feet disaster and drama
Are making a second-rate movie.
Take no notice my darling Mr. B.
Tell me a simple answer to the urgent question:
Who am I? Who are we?

Mr. B. is a known madman—a suspected murderer.
I think the cops are after him for being himself;
For not sobbing, for not beating his breast
When he finds a victim on the beach,
Bloody and wet in the tide.
Was that my body we saw down there Mr. B.?
Twisted in seaweed? Who am I? Who was I?

He picked me up on the beach.

I am the tiny, tiny girl in the thin nightgown
That Mr. B. carries curled in a seashell
In his trousers' pocket, among
The sticks of Dentyne gum and the spent flashbulbs.
Oh I am glad I am dead and can't see
The dirty darkness in here.
I was murdered last Thursday, but even so
The heat of his groin and all the fumbling that goes on there
Is disturbing my final rest.

# *Ian Tyson*

## FOUR STRONG WINDS

> Four strong winds that blow lonely,
> Seven seas that run high,
> All those things that don't change come what may—
> But our good times are all gone
> And I'm bound for movin' on,
> I'll look for you if I'm ever back this way—

I think I'll go out to Alberta—
Weather's good there in the fall,
I got some friends that I can go to workin' for—
Still I wish you'd change your mind
If I asked you one more time
But we've been through that a hundred times or more—

> Four strong winds that blow lonely,
> Seven seas that run high,
> All those things that don't change come what may—
> But our good times are all gone
> And I'm bound for movin' on,
> I'll look for you if I'm ever back this way—

If I get there before the snow flies
And if things are goin' good,
You could meet me if I sent you down the fare.
But, by then it would be winter,
Ain't too much for you to do
And those winds sure can blow cold way out there.

> Four strong winds that blow lonely,
> Seven seas that run high
> All those things that don't change come what may—
> But our good times are all gone
> And I'm bound for movin' on,
> I'll look for you if I'm ever back this way—

# *Tom Wayman*

## THE DOW RECRUITER, or
## This Young Man Is Making Up His Mind

They're always playing tricks on me, by
telling me their name is Eichmann, or
they're really interested in our
gas project—the one for Zyklon-B.
Others are earnest, showing me those—
those photographs of the children and
appealing to me as a man, how
can one work for the company if
it is like that. Others say the creeps
outside don't bother them, they just want
to work for something settled, with plans.
And there are those who take the folders
thoughtfully, as I did, thinking too
of the God-damned crying child.
Flowers,
bright red ones along the lane, turn just
one side to the sun, one face of their
mass of petals. What a man is, is
less clear, and what a man is doing . . .
Violence overflows, the shouting and
the bodies crowd in sometimes, the red-
faced officials saying things to me
and all those people. My wife keeps our
bedsheets cool and quiet, now that the
money comes. Sundays, the green spread and
the white room hold the lights, and outside
red flowers are growing in the lane.

THE SEASON OF EDEN

Softly the sun mentions
—fifteen
there are fifteen winds.

O and which one is it
then, ruffling her hair,
the sweet brown threads spreading
in a rippling webbing?

The sun insists
on the season

and that all winds but four
were lost in Eden
and whisper themselves to themselves
over the earth's ranges,
slip down to circle the slim form
of beauty, wherever it is Eve:
loved before desire

—the sun says
of her litheness, quick
eyes, bright smooth wriggly body—
eleven, eleven caress her
until the moment
of despair for her gentleness
or the necessary crash of sweat.

# *Ian Young*

## FEAR OF THE LANDSCAPE

On a hot morning
walking through rough thicket,
bushes and rocks
close to the bluffs
I was uneasy and clung to things.
The sound of a cricket
or the calls of birds were shrill
lesions in the quiet air
around me, sweltering and still.
The leaves hung from the trees
dangling on thin stems.

I am walking quickly and the land
stops. The ground
drops to a beach of stones
where a silent boat leans at the shore
into a sandy mound,
its stiff poled oars
outstretched.
The lake gulls circling it
cry out in the heat.
The sound of dry breath clings to me.
I hear the sun's core burn.
Have I been too long in cities
that I have such fear
of the landscape?

# NOTES

# *Milton Acorn*

## ISLANDERS

The Island referred to is Prince Edward in the Gulf of St. Lawrence. I think what the writer is saying in the first verse is that you'd never guess the occupation of these men from their appearance. They are friendly and cheerful men, who face danger every day and take their lunch cans to work. Do you know any other people who resemble this description of fishermen? What is the writer really saying in the second verse? The fishermen's forebears lived even more dangerous lives, siring sons of a proud and independent nature. Does it seem a bit tame now that the old rum-running days are gone? The writer didn't mean the end of this poem to be funny, but when it is read aloud most people laugh. Do you think it is funny? For myself, I think it's sad as well as funny.

## I'VE TASTED MY BLOOD TOO MUCH

Milton Acorn was deeply involved in socialist politics when I knew him in Montreal. From reading what happened to the writer's mother and his friends, can socialism be justified? Or is it that simple? Do you think the writer goes slightly overboard with his promise to "change things" at the end of the poem? Or is he completely justified in his anger? Underneath the rhetoric in the poem (but it's pretty good rhetoric) do you feel the same idealism in the writer as I do? Is there really any answer to such injustices at all? Is it possible for you to feel as Acorn does?

## "CALLUM"

What is a "Pusher"? I'd say some kind of foreman, but I'm not sure if it's a real term or an Acorn invention. Do you think there is any connection between the writer remembering "Callum" and not knowing which "Island" he came from? I think the effect is to universalize the dead man, make him more myth than man. Do you think there's any idealization involved in the description and character of "Callum"?

## SKY'S POEM FOR CHRISTMAS

As a matter of interest, Sky was the small son of one of Acorn's friends. The poem strikes me as a sort of personal war between belief and disbelief; an affirmation of self that contains some really inspired rhetoric. Jupiter (that's Roman, Zeus is the Greek original) was the king-pin god of the Greeks, and took over the job from an older crueller pantheon of gods. Do you think it's possible, considering the number of new stars come into being over the centuries, that one of them did signify the birth of a miraculous child? Acorn is saying that by the law of averages, since so many wonderful things did happen, this event could have happened as well. Isn't that rather faulty logic? Are the possibilities really limitless? Do you think children retain more faith and belief than adults? It's probable that Acorn wore a beard and red suit and played Santa Claus for the boy, Sky, at Christmas. If so, Acorn himself received the gifts mentioned. Would you agree with this interpretation? The writer caught a glimpse of himself as the boy saw him, and acting out the myth of Santa Claus made him realize that he too was a myth and symbol to himself as a human being. Do you agree with this?

## KNOWING I LIVE IN A DARK AGE

The title comes from a poem by Bertolt Brecht, a very famous playwright and communist who died in East Germany several years ago. Implicit in that "dark age" idea is the faith that the world will eventually get better and things will be much improved. Do you think this is true? Why do you or don't you? Do you think the world has improved in the last hundred or thousand years? Acorn seems to believe there is a basic honesty in people (as exemplified by the newsboy), a thought with which I do not necessarily agree. Do *you* think people are basically honest? Why should they be? Could they be—in the world as it is today? The contrast of bullying crows and cruel wolves is set against the self-sacrifice of Jesus. Suppose Jesus had been an ordinary man and not "the son of God", do you think he would have obtained any satisfaction from his own martyrdom? Even if he did, was it worthwhile? In the last verse Acorn says things are pretty bad all over, and that writing poems doesn't help much. He thinks I am a cynic, but suspects me of his own idealism underneath the cynicism. He wants to make the world different than what it is and myself different from what he thinks I am. Do you agree with him that things are pretty bad all over? Does idealism help the individual or the world? Jean Paul Sartre has a philosophy whose gist is that man invents himself from day to day, that everything a person does changes his own personality. Acorn apparently believes that writing a poem changes the poet. Is this true?

### AT EL CORTIJO

El Cortijo is or was—I don't know if it's still operating—a Montreal coffee house. People there played chess, guitars, drank coffee, and talked—mostly talked. Do you think the girl selecting the writer's knee for a "public perch" was accidental or deliberate? What would you do in a similar situation, depending on whether you are a boy or girl? What do you think was going on at El Cortijo that so fascinated the girl? After the poem ended, what do you think might have happened?

## *Margaret Atwood*

### DREAMS OF THE ANIMALS

Does it seem extraordinary to you that animals might have dreams? Assuming that they do have dreams, do the dreams ascribed to them by Margaret Atwood seem to be the natural ones each particular animal might have? Why should mice and small rodents "have nightmares of a huge pink/shape with five claws descending"? Why should birds dream of "territories"? Why are soap and metal said to be evil? Why should the armadillo be insane? In the poem the free animals dream of other animals, whereas the caged animals' dreams are in connection with their immediate environment. Does the writer mean to convey anything by the difference in dreams of caged and free animals?

## AT THE TOURIST CENTRE IN BOSTON

Does it seem to you that the writer herself is partly deceived by this manufactured illusion of her own country? When she says, "Who really lives there?", does she mean: who lives in Canada?; or who lives in this tourist model? What does the poet mean by the citizens planning "odd red massacres"? Could this be related to the Indian wars, or are all massacres "red"? For myself, I have an impression that this model of Canada makes the author uneasy, and she isn't entirely sure that the country might not be only a collection of empty houses where no one lives. Do you think Americans get an accurate impression of Canada from such models, or are they only advertising?

## BACKDROP ADDRESSES COWBOY

This poem is about the violent tradition in the U.S., from the actual cowboy to television series, etc., etc. Do you think that the "violent people" are aware of other people watching them, or are in any way affected by other people's opinions? Does the writer actually say that the violent people do things that can never be undone? Are there some things that can't be lassoed or controlled in any way? Could it be that the "I" of the poem is really the earth, the watching conscious world?

# *Earle Birney*

## THE BEAR ON THE DELHI ROAD

Do the Kashmiri men in this poem wish to make the bear more human? After the bear has learned to dance would it be possible for him to go back to his previous peaceful berry-picking existence? After human beings have learned something, gone through any particular human experience at all, are they exactly the same people as they were before? In other words, do you think experience changes people? Is there any cruelty in the men's treatment of the bear? What does Birney mean by "free myth from reality"? Is there a sense in which men too are helpless and have no control over what they do? If this is so, would you say it also applies to people like Eichmann and any other murderer? Could you apply it to yourself, or do you feel responsible for the things you do?

## TWENTY-THIRD FLIGHT

Where do you think Birney got the method for writing this poem? Does it sound familiar to you? Does Birney appear to care very much that what appears might happen that night will not actually happen? Do you think it should happen?

## MEETING OF STRANGERS

Do you think the bicyclist in the poem was really going to rob Birney? Assuming that he was, what do you feel is the attitude expressed by "dat a nice jump you got too"? Would you feel the same as Birney did in a similar situation?

## CANADA: CASE HISTORY

Do you think Canada is a "highschool land" and has not yet reached maturity? In every way? What is maturity in the case of a country like Canada? Does the "Uncle" spoil the Canadian child by pampering it at table, but refuse to listen if the child speaks up? Do you think Canadians actually do dream of "winning the global race"? Should they? The unmarried parents are, of course, France and Britain. Who does Birney refer to when he says the relatives are "keen to bag the estate"? How does schizophrenia come into it? If Canada has not reached maturity, when will it be too late? Too late for what?

## THE MAMMOTH CORRIDORS

Using excerpts from an imaginary guidebook for satiric comment, Earle Birney describes a trip from west to east by car, which is perhaps also a description of his own life, including Canadian history and geology. What and where is the "great island"? Is there any contrast in your opinion between the character of people mentioned and the landscape itself? What does Birney mean by "the spastic traffic of buyers and bought"? Hasn't commerce always been buying and selling? Do you think describing his car as "the master I own" indicates the relationship between car-owners and their cars. Is it possible for a car to own a man? How? Birney describes Indians trailing mammoths down melting corridors in the ice-cap about 10,000 years ago. Can you form a visual impression in your own mind from his description? What are "the truths that compel" Birney? In this poem "the point of no return" is after the Indians have gone far enough in their mammoth-hunt that they cannot return because there is no food on their back-trail. They must kill the mammoths for food, else starve to death. Do you ever feel that humanity has reached the point of no return, though perhaps in a different way? If so, in what way? Birney mentions that everything has changed greatly since he was born. Do you think he feels comfortable with all these changes? Will you be in another fifty years? The "Greenland lodger" refers to the still-existing glaciers of the north. At the poem's end does Birney imply that there may be another ice age in the future? Or does he mean something else?

## *bill bissett*

### NUCLEAR CIRCULAR

Bill Bissett, a young Vancouver poet, believes that language itself has grown stale and worn-out over the years, and that it must be re-vitalized by such novelties as odd spelling, strange combinations of words, etc. Some people are antagonized by such devices in poetry—are you? Even if you do dislike, say, the spelling (in which Bissett is not particularly consistent), do you feel that his poems may have some merit just the same, if you are able to struggle thru to understanding them? In this poem Bissett seems to say that people as people mean very little to governments, and even to other people. And now that the either/or proposition of staying in Vancouver or leaving it in the event of nuclear attack is presented to him, he realizes that he has turned away from more things than he has held onto— What does that mean? And what does he mean by saying the typewriter is breaking down on him? Why does he want to reach the people who printed the circular? Why is the threatening bomb a "symbol of our hesitancies"?

## POEM

This piece strikes me as a fantasy with quite serious undertones. Again we have Bissett's unusual spelling, and his ability to take very ordinary things and make them something more than that. Do you think that the God in this poem might be interchangeable with someone else in a position of authority? What does Bissett mean by saying, "i think they had the line removd"? Could the poem be described in any way as a social poem? Does it seem a little childish? For instance, when you were a child did you ever imagine a little man that made things go, inside motor cars and washing machines? The little man from the sewing machine told them what it was like to live there. Are you curious about the way other people live, whether or not inside sewing machines?

# *George Bowering*

## ESTA MUY CALIENTE

Bowering writes in a deliberately plain style, as much like ordinary speech as possible. His poems may even sound flat, and never melodramatic; he allows the bare statement of what happened to stand by itself and make the poem. The picture of Mexican life presented here is that of a very poor people, and may be thought slightly depressing. Do you think this is a true picture of Mexico? One could never imagine a whole town turning out for someone's funeral in Canada. Why do you think this was the case in Mexico? What is Bowering's point in the last verse? We know very well that it is hot for both Mexicans and Canadians: why is this point emphasized?

## THE CANADA COUNCIL POET

This piece might be called an "in" poem: that is, only poets are liable to appreciate it fully. Being called a "true poet" is one of the clichés among poets. (Irving Layton has the habit of calling the verse of a young poet "very lively") What do you think Bowering means when he says he hadn't seen the "Canada Council Poet" in the police station? Is there an implication that having received Canada Council Fellowships (money that buys academics and others time to write) is harmful to a writer? And yet nearly every country in the world with any literary pretensions has set up a system of such fellowships. Is it possible that both these writers are jabbing each other verbally? Is one liable to write better poems if one frequents book stores, universities and liquor stores? Or the man who lives a harder and more adventurous life, where hands get blistered, people sweat and get dirty at their jobs—is this man likely to do better work? Or does that have anything to do with it? Does the poem seem trivial?

## *Jim Brown*

### PORTRAIT

Do you ever feel there are extraordinary qualities about another person, as the writer does about the girl in the poem? Jim Brown portrays a person here with qualities we think do not normally go together. If you were the writer, would you mention both crooked teeth and amazing eyes, or should both be mentioned? How would you describe such a person as this girl, using different words than Brown's?

## *Ivan Burgess*

### AS HE LAY DYING

Does this poem seem a good description of the outward circumstances of death? Could it fit any other situation? In the last verse: who expected the silence? Is there any hint of criticism here? After the person's death, does it seem ordinary to you that several voices rose at once, "like a sprung mouse trap"? Is there any hint of affection or love in the speaker's description of the scene, or it is just description? Do you think the poem is more or less typical of all such scenes of death?

# *Leonard Cohen*

## FOR E. P. J.

This poem amounts to a series of images. It shows the writer as a kind of dreamy moony person who seems to live in some other time than now. I think it's very difficult to sum up the poem, and say what it is all about, in fact I would never try. However, do you like such lines as "I once believed a single line/in a Chinese poem could change/forever how blossoms fell"? Is that line beautiful or not? I don't know what beauty is either, and knowing a thing is beautiful won't help you to tell why it is. One must call such a poem romantic, and some have called Cohen's poems decadent. "Decadent" here because the writer is preoccupied with past things to the near exclusion of the present. What does Cohen mean when he says "Something forgets us perfectly"? Would it be a good thing if a writer always wrote in this fashion?

# *John Robert Colombo*

## THE FRENCH IN QUEBEC

This poem is taken directly from the published prose of William Lyon Mackenzie, who was the leader of the 1837 rebellion in Upper Canada and later became the first mayor of Toronto. This poem is "compiled," one might say, rather than written. Colombo has appropriated it as his own, while giving Mackenzie credit for the original authorship. What do you think of the idea of using other people's prose as your own poems? The popular name for this sort of thing is "found poems." Are you interested in what Mackenzie had to say about French and English Canadians 130 years ago? Do any of the present-day political parties in Canada seem to agree with what Mackenzie says here? Or have things changed since the old red-haired rebel's hey-day? Does this poem mean anything to you right now, have contemporary relevance?

# *Frank Davey*

## THE FACT

The poem is a description of what happens all the time, a girl sitting beside a man in a car and shifting gears for him. One supposes they are in love. Do you think they are? Why? Why is the night "slatted"? George Bowering and Frank Davey are both said to be followers of a particular school of poetry, the Black Mountain Group, originating in the U.S., and hence each of them might be said to write like the other. Is that true? Do Bowering's and Davey's poems resemble each other in any way? Do you think it's a good thing to be a "follower" of some school or other, take someone else as your example?

# *Kildare Dobbs*

## SONG FOR CONFORMISTS

The point of this poem hits you over the head with a club. Nobody, not me, not you, not even a teacher could miss the point. Okay, is it a good thing to be a non-conformist? Always? If you are always a non-conformist, you go to bed at different times, never arrive at the right hour for appointments, you talk back to the boss if you have one, you disagree with what other people say. In fact you lead quite a hectic existence. It isn't possible to be like that all the time, is it? Reason and moderation in all things as the old saying goes. But reason and moderation lead to conformity, don't they? Just as non-conformity leads to chaos. So how do you figure it all out?

# *Louis Dudek*

## INSCRIPTIONS

It may sound funny, but this poem always gives me a little shiver somewhere when I read it. Maybe it's just the thought that the people who made love and the "captain of hosts in Sinai" have been dead and dust for several thousand years. But why did the captain of hosts write his inscription on a wall so long ago? If you've ever written on a wall or tree yourself, why did you do it? Is it that all of us want to live forever, that we want to leave something of ourselves behind when we go? Or now? Is the poem in some way sad, or does it make you feel good? Like me, does it give you that little shiver?

# *R. G. Everson*

## WHEN I'M GOING WELL

This poem is a picture of a man who, for whatever reason, is elated and feeling joyful. His mind makes fantasies at the Westmount Glen railway in Montreal. Sparks from the railway engine are like the laughing brides in Breughel paintings. (Breughel was an old Dutch painter who specialized in painting ordinary people). The idea of the poem may be that the man can do just about anything, his mind allows him to think anything. Does this come across to you when you read the poem? It's a fantasy with a solid base in reality, for what could be more real than a railway station! Have you ever felt so exultant and joyful that your mind made fantasies? What form would yours take?

## *Doug Fetherling*

### NIGHT BEFORE LAST

Where do you think the events of this wild night took place? Do you think, on reading the poem, that it is necessary to take an attitude of either approval or disapproval? Or should it simply be regarded as a poem, in which certain things happened to certain other people? Can you think of any reason why the writer should have dreamed of Carl Sandburg, the American poet, after the party?

## *Robert Finch*

### CAMPERS

Another poem that hits you over the head with its point. The writer says everything changes; as of course, it does; and that nothing is permanent; and he's right. But you can't worry about that all the time, can you? What Finch is saying is that a person must prepare himself mentally for change and know that it's going to happen. On the other hand there is some kind of philosophical tag that goes "Live your life as if you were going to live forever". So who's right? Finch or that last bit of philosophy? While we're alive there is one thing that can be relatively permanent, which is part of the body and mind of the person concerned. One more or less permanent thing—what is it? Why not grow to a wall, because even if it falls, as you know it must sooner or later, there must be loyalties and brief areas of permanence in a human lifetime.

# *Len Gasparini*

## COLD-WATER FLAT BLUES

Do you know anyone like the guy in this poem? Do you think his life is really the way he describes, or is he romantically exaggerating? What do you think he does with his time, other than starving to death? Is he an artist or writer? Is he a hippie? Or just an ordinary guy trying to get along in the world? He says he's a poet in the last verse. Is that true? Is the poem up-beat in tone? Or is it defeatist?

# *Eldon Grier*

## TONY AT SEA

Is the Tony of the poem trying to change his bride in some way? If so, why doesn't he like her the way she is? If you met a guy like this would you admire him or just walk away? What's wrong with imitating other people? Do you ever do that? Is it cruel sometimes? Tony is a comedian—at least Grier makes him sound like one—and wants to break into the sadness of his preoccupied wife. Does that sound accurate? Do laughter and sadness ever go together? Do you think Tony should succeed, so his wife will be no longer sad? When a person is sad they sometimes want to be left alone, as Tony's bride does. But if they are nearly always sad and blue should another person try to break into their sadness? Should a husband?

## BURY ME IN MY CADILLAC

The man in this poem has achieved success, owns all the trappings. But is that all there is to it? What is success? Money, power, love? Is there anything else? Can a person travelling on the road to success ever turn back? Can anyone ever turn back, no matter what road he is on?

# *George Johnston*

## THE ROLL CALL

George Johnston is a humourous writer who loves some of the odd characteristics and habits of people, while at the same time satirizing them in outrageous verse. Do you think such a poem as this should be taken seriously? For one does take a humourous poem seriously, sometimes. Do you think the roll call of his aunts really comforts Johnston? How could their names comfort him when he so obviously pokes fun at them? Do you think he also pokes fun at himself? What does he mean by his "wormy shelves and cupboards"? What other "crumbling things" does he have to keep?

## WAR ON THE PERIPHERY

It strikes me that here Johnston is noting the thin line between gentleness and violence. Would you say he is more afraid that his family might be vulnerable to the "violent, obedient ones"?—or that he fears his family itself might turn into the thing he fears. Why are the violent ones, said to be so obedient? What do they obey? What do you think of the sort of life that Johnston says he lives? Does it seem to you that he says one either lives that peaceful sheltered life, or else the violent life? Do you think Johnston exaggerates the dangers in this poem? Can pleasure be, as he describes it, "discreet"? Does this portrait he gives of himself sound like that of a typical Canadian? Or is there really such a thing as a typical Canadian?

# *George Jonas*

## PEACE

Do you believe, as Jonas says, that "There is no conflict that love or bullets/Could not resolve in time"? In the fourth verse various animals act as if someone very powerful had declared an armistice for all things. Do you think it's possible that animals could ever stop preying on each other, no matter what the reason for the stoppage might be? Whether animals can or not, we do know that there are periods of peace among the human beings: therefore, how would you compare humans to animals in this regard? In the sixth verse, as a result of peace, some rather amazing and beautiful things happen. If peace continued, would these warm and beneficial things also continue? Do you agree with Jonas when he says "The beauty of such moments is hardly useful"? At the end of the poem, has the writer actually made a "positive statement" about peace or not? Who are the old men who "sit at tables"?

# *Lionel Kearns*

## APPOINTMENT

What does Kearns mean by the "nightmare dog-pack"? Does he mean the dog-pack would destroy the homes if they turned on them? What is the "black slit" that opens in the sky? What, if anything, is about to happen to the little boy climbing from the abandoned bus?

# *A. M. Klein*

## FRIGIDAIRE

Do you think it's possible to see the inside of a refrigerator as a village in Quebec? Why not? A city brilliantly lit up at night might be said to look like a glass chandelier. Is this the same way of seeing things as Klein uses in his poem? What does he mean by the storm with its "muffled thunder"? When Klein says this sight is "exclusive" and "secret", does he mean that it's only possible for *him* to look inside his frigidaire, and that no one else can? Or does he mean that only himself can see a Laurentian village inside? Do you think it's a good think to see both the thing itself and something else at the same time?

### POLITICAL MEETING

Have you personally ever heard a speaker who could convince you of nearly anything? In your own case, which speakers have the most influence on you? Do they have any qualities in common with this political speaker? Do you generally believe what they say? The orator in this poem is making a point that English-speaking Canadians have imposed conscription during wartime in Canada, and that they did so in Quebec because they are English and dislike Quebeckers. Do you know what percentage of English-speaking Canadians are of English descent? Do you think that political victories may sometimes be won by playing off one of the two founding races against each other? Would you regard this as legitimate?

## *Frederick E. Laight*

### DROUGHT

This poem has been included in many previous anthologies. The reason I also included it here is that it is one of the very few good ones about the depression, the so-called "Hungry Thirties." I was a youngster during those years myself, and went through them scarcely realizing what was happening, the agonies of hunger and frustration people were experiencing. But Laight realizes it fully. Does that first verse make one think of abandonment, of empty cities and countryside? What would the wagons be loaded with? Do you think statesmen are often "bowed with cares"? Or do they seem more concerned with getting votes and their own comforts? Would rain have solved all the crop failures, lack of jobs, etc.? Does the mood of the poem's writer sound rather hopeless? Can we ourselves actually realize what people felt during the depression?

# *Archibald Lampman*

## MORNING ON THE LIEVRE

What sort of atmosphere do you think Lampman creates in the first two verses of this poem? Do you think the flight of ducks in their precise formation, or the screaming jay, weaken or destroy this atmosphere? The poem was written near the end of the last century: do you think anything like it could or would be written today? Do you know of any places similar to that described in the poem?

# *Pat Lane*

## ELEPHANTS

This is a modern poem, but like Laight's "Drought" it too creates a rather hopeless mood. Do you think the writer likes his job from the sound of it? If you had the same job can you imagine circumstances in which the job would be interesting? How do you feel about such things as Indian graveyards being lost and buried under highways? How would the Indians like it? Is there any real parallel between the elephant graveyard and the Indians' graveyard, apart from the fact that both cannot be found?

# *Ernest Lanigan*

## A THRENODY

I think this is one of the funniest poems I've ever read. However, there are things about the poem that require prior-to-reading awareness of them for more complete enjoyment. For instance, what well-known poet wrote a line similar to "Swats wha' hae wi' Ahkoond bled"? What other poet wrote a serious poem mourning the death of a great man? The quality of saying something seriously and not-seriously at the same time might be called "tongue-in-cheek". Do you ever talk to your friends this way? It's my personal belief that if you attempt to explain a poem enough you destroy any possible enjoyment on the part of the reader. Have I managed to do that in this poem? The author really takes nothing very seriously, including death and the sorrowing subjects of the "Ahkoond". Do you think that, once in a while, this attitude towards life is helpful when things get difficult?

# *Irving Layton*

## COMPOSITION IN LATE SPRING

Why does the writer feel so exultant that the downtown street and people seem so different to what they usually are? Does this seem to you similar to a basic personality change? Or would the writer generally be the sort of person he describes himself to be in the poem? Are the "damned ones" those who don't feel as Layton does? If so, do you think they should be damned for this reason? Why do you think Layton feels he has defeated death?

## HOW POEMS GET WRITTEN

What could Layton mean by "a memory torn at the shoulders"? By writing this poem together, does he mean writing it in their life and actions?

## THE SATYR

There is in this poem, to me, a suggestion that time itself can somehow be conquered and made nothing by love. Do you think this could be true in any way, or is it just poet's nonsense? I think there is also a light-hearted quality about the poem which is meant to apply to love itself. Do you think love is light-hearted, or that it can and should be?

### ON SEEING THE STATUETTES OF EZEKIEL AND JEREMIAH

What seems strange to me is that a couple of Hebrew minor prophets of some 5,000 years ago have emerged from a Near Eastern desert to become characters in Irving's Layton's poem. It's almost as if he were talking to living people in this poem. Do you think the two saints can possibly be comforted by Layton's reassurances? Or is it himself he is somehow trying to comfort? Is it a religious poem? Do you think that talking to Ezekiel and Jeremiah is a desperate move on Layton's part, and that he feels alienated from his surroundings? Do you think that the "arrogant men" (probably clerks in office buildings) are better company than priests for the two saints?

### TO THE GIRLS OF MY GRADUATING CLASS

Do you think Layton gives an accurate picture of young girls? He seems to say they have opposite and opposing qualities. Is this true? Is there really so much difference between the two generations of youth and middle age? Is Layton really ridiculous when he says "hobbles after you a little way"? Is this funny?

## *Dennis Lee*

### 400: COMING HOME

This is a poem about a hitch-hiker, that is very obvious. But can the hitch-hiker be anyone else than he seems to be? Why does Lee describe the fields as waiting "patiently as though someone/believed in them"? On the face of it, that's a ridiculous thing to say about fields, why then did he say it? To pursue the subject a little further: do people and things have to be believed in for any reason you can think of? The writer says that many of the things he lived for are falling apart, and he mentions rock music, hondas, beer on porches etc.—then says that isn't what he means. What does he mean? Or is there any way of coming at what he does mean? Or could it all be meaningless? One line keeps getting repeated: "You are still on the highway." What motive could the writer have for this repetition?

## HE ASKS HER

In this poem the writer tells the girls all his triumphs, the stories that reflect credit on himself. But do they really reflect credit on him? Or, if they did once, do they still? We, the collective reader, are not told all the facts of this situation. We are not exactly sure why the girl would be "cast down again" or why the man "would be rejected." The writer wonders what kind of pickle he and the girl were in. How would you answer that? Of course these little triumphs themselves were not enough of themselves: they had to be told to someone, a girl in this case. Do you yourself have this habit, of telling your triumphs to someone you love or respect? Is it boasting or do you expect a natural interest on the part of the other person? Where do you draw the line between "boasting" and "natural interest"?

# *Malcolm Lowry*

## CHRIST WALKS IN THIS INFERNAL DISTRICT TOO

The title of this piece reminds me of Dante's "Inferno," though I can't be sure if that's what Lowry had in mind. I knew Lowry briefly in Vancouver, years ago. A friend and I went to visit him at his shack on Burrard Inlet, and drank most of the evening (soft drinks of course). Lowry was red-faced, alcoholic and fascinating to me. I sat copying poems of his I particularly liked by the light of a coal-oil lamp, while Lowry and my friend splashed in the evening-blue water. In the poem he talks of Canada as if we have a choice in its development or ruin. Do you think we actually do have this choice? Incidentally, Lowry himself was haunted by guilt and despair and penury most of his life. He didn't believe he had any choice personally. Yet he thinks that Canada has one? Isn't that odd?

## WITHOUT THE NIGHTED WYVERN

Are notions of freedom really tied up with drink? Lowry's ideal life contained a tavern: what does your ideal life contain? I think Lowry may be satirizing himself here, since it strikes me highly unlikely that the best he could desire is a better tavern. The business of "Weaving the vision of the unassimilable inn" strikes me as a paradox, since he has already imagined the inn he sits in in order to imagine other and better inns. Isn't that rather absurd? Or is it? It's like the picture on the cornflakes box that contains another picture that contains another picture that contains another picture and so on. Could Lowry mean that we don't know what we want, or that we always want the unattainable?

### OLD FREIGHTER IN AN OLD PORT

When Lowry was 17 years old he left his well-to-do family and friends and sailed on deep-sea freighters all over the world. As a result of these experiences he later wrote the novel, "Ultramarine" and many poems about the sea. It's obvious that when one has been a long time away from home one is lonely and wants news of friends and relations. Therefore, the first place visited when a ship reached port was likely to be the postoffice. Would you feel that way if you were a 17-year old seaman? Can you identify either of the two novels Lowry takes the poem's closing images from? In its simplest terms, Lowry feels good in the morning. Why?

## *Pat Lowther*

### ON READING A POEM WRITTEN IN ADOLESCENCE

Many people remember childhood with regret for the past that is gone, and dislike the present which is not all they think it should be. Do you see any signs of this attitude in Pat Lowther's poem? The poem seems to say there were once many more things to enjoy, and new things to feel and see. Does it really say that? What is meant by "how many hands I had/hooked in the sky"? Why the sky and not the earth? Do you think the writer's entire past is irretrievably lost?

# *L. A. Mackay*

## SNOW STORY

This is a mood poem, and the mood is mystery and suspense. One can't explain it in any terms of logic and reality. If you have ever read De la Mare's "The Listeners," I think you'll notice a similarity of mood. There is also a resemblance to a poem of Earl Birney's (not included here) called "Bushed." Reading the poem one's mind throngs with questions. Why was the man moving stealthily on snowshoes towards the cabin? Was it his own cabin or a strange place? What was it that killed him? But it's no use to ask any of these questions, at least I don't think so. One simply accepts the mood and mystery of the poem and lets it go at that. If you try to get a logical interpretation you'll end up in the loony-ward. But the mood, the mood is lovely.

# *Alexander McLachlan*

## THE DEATH OF THE OX

McLachlan's original poem (pub. 1888) was re-written and modernized by the present editor, while retaining as much of his meaning and intent as possible. McLachlan's feelings about his ox might be compared to Earle Birney's remark that his car is "the master I own", to Alden Nowlan's "The boys sport leather jackets and levis,/but that's their underwear,/the car is their real clothing—" Could you carry the comparison any further? For one thing, a car is replaceable if you have the money, but McLachlan felt his ox could not be replaced because he could not love another animal in the same way. McLachlan came here from Scotland in 1840, and cleared land in the forests of Upper Canada. At that time the great trees dominated everything. Not just farms and people, not only log cabins and roads. Wherever you lived in those scattered British colonies in the year of our Lord, A.D. 1840, the forest was always at the edge of your vision. If you ventured away from the small clearings, sunlight filtered down through soughing green branches in a perpetual twilight. At night in the deep woods of Upper Canada the moon and stars were twice removed, first beyond the forest and then past light years of space and time. Could you imagine yourself as such a pioneer, if not in the early forests then as an astronaut on a strange planet? Do you think those pioneers were much different than we are today? If so, how? I mean basically, apart from living in a woods clearing and having to work very hard. What satisfactions do you think they got out of life? Apparently the companionship of an ox was one satisfaction for McLachlan, but can you think of others?

# *Annette & Jim Murray*

## BENOIT

Jim and Annette Murray are folksingers who lived for years in Montreal, now in Vancouver. This song resulted from a friend visiting them, and recounting some of the difficulties of his everyday life in Quebec. The friend's name, of course, was "Benoit." The principal theme of both song and Jean Benoit himself is language, the French language. Some of his difficulties seem a little comic on the printed page, or while listening to Jim Murray sing the song on the record (Melbourne (Rodeo) AMLP 4005), but are they really so comic? Does Jean Benoit have reasonable grounds for believing that—in his own homeland of Quebec—even in the most important situations he cannot be understood sometimes and may be discriminated against because of his language? In the song's first French interpolation, Benoit says his home is Canada, "et je suis content de ça—which translates as: "and I'm pleased that this is so." Therefore Benoit is pleased to be a Canadian, but not pleased when forced to speak English in the French province of Quebec. Is that reasonable? What about Italian, German and Hungarian immigrants—should they be required to speak English only? Or is that a good and valid comparison? What about Indians and Eskimos? Canada was their homeland before it was ours—should it be necessary that all of them speak English? In other words, can Canada remain a nation if its various component peoples all continue to speak their original languages? Or should there be only the two principal languages, French and English? Do you think it's likely that after Benoit had nearly completed a course in engineering he was told: "No Frenchmen here"? It does seem a bit exaggerated to me. However, even if there are such exaggerations among French Canadians, are they entirely unreasonable in wanting French to be the official language of Quebec? If they are unhappy with the language situation as it is, does the rest of Canada have any obligation to make improvements?

It probably has no significance that "Benoit" was based on an old English folk song called "Sam Hall." And that song derives from a still earlier one called "Jack Hall," which commemorated the hanging of Jack Hall, a chimney sweep, in London for burglary and murder in 1701. Before execution he was allowed to speak, and his hatred of the world was expressed with cordial vehemence and well-chosen cuss-words. The musical version runs—in brief—like this: "My name it is Sam Hall/and I hate you one and all/Damn your eyes!" Do you find it curious that an English folk song is now used to express a French Canadian point of view about the French language in Canada?

# *John Newlove*

## THEN, IF I CEASE DESIRING

I first met Newlove when he lived in a cleared space in the middle of a pottery factory under Granville Bridge in Vancouver. He writes his own life into his poems, much the same as I do though we are very different poets. But I wouldn't be a bit surprised if at one time Newlove stole cars and travelled the highways drunkenly. Does this poem remind you, even a little, of the tone of voice and feeling in Leonard Cohen's poem earlier in this book? What Newlove seems to say here is that he wants time itself, the actual thing that happened, and not praise or monuments. Do you agree with this? And yet we encounter the paradox of the writer saying such moments are really very little. What does he mean?

## THE FLOWERS

Is there any implication in the poem that Newlove's brother was hit by a police car? Or was it just another hit-and-run driver? Do you believe in mercy-killing? i.e., what kind of miserable existence in hospital did this man have, and was there any point in continuing such an existence? The poem gives a picture of night and rain on the city streets. How do you feel about that? Does the picture seem right and in focus? What does Newlove mean by his "flowery clock."

## A LETTER TO LARRY SEALEY, 1962

This poem seems to me like the diary of a hitch-hiker. Nothing in life, at least no material thing can be held onto when one leads that sort of life. Does the writer's attitude seem to have an element of desperation in it? If so, why? The whole thing is almost unreal, complete fantasy. I rode the freight trains during the depression, and I think of my box-car experiences the same way. I remember, I know I was there, but it doesn't seem quite real. Why is this? What "ostentation" is there, scribbling on paper towels? Why do you think he felt happy? Does the whole poem through its jerky terse rhythms give you a sense of rushing movement. A writer named Jack Kerouac writes of "The Road" in somewhat romantic terms: do you think Newlove is romantic? I note that some people think my own freight train experiences were romantic, but they weren't to me at that time, they were just thunder of iron rails, dirt and cinders, knocking on doors for handouts, and so on. But perhaps what happens in the past assumes this romantic tinge. Does your own past seem somehow weird or wonderful, or quite ordinary?

## NOT MOVING

Another hitch-hiking poem. The point is so obvious that I'm afraid to talk about it at all. Besides, I dislike this analysis and dissection of poems. It amounts to that, even if you only ask questions about them. The questions should be silent in your own mind, and the answers you get change every time you look at the poem. However, apart from the activity of hitch-hiking, there are other times in people's lives when they stop and look around at things, wondering where they're going and why. Have you ever stopped in the middle of what you're doing, just wondering, perhaps like Newlove cold and afraid? Or perhaps walking in the woods, have you ever tried to imagine the animals not far away, the birds and insects? The multitudinous activity around you?

# *Alden Nowlan*

## IN THE HAINESVILLE CEMETERY

Alden Nowlan is a large and gracefully ungainly man who grew up in New Brunswick, works on the editorial staff of a Saint John, N.B. newspaper, and chronicles the lives and characters of maritime people with love and acid. Have you ever met people like the Talbots in this poem—the ultra-cautious type who look so long before they leap they may never leap? On the other hand, isn't there something solid and admirable about such people? Do you think Nowlan is right in his implication that Mary anticipates her own death by putting a jar of flowers on her future grave? Can such people enjoy the world they're in now, if they're continually looking forward to another world?

## SATURDAY NIGHT

Is Nowlan right in saying "the car is their real clothing"? Why do you think they act like that? Is it showing off for the girls? Do you ever do anything similar? Could this portrait be one of a small town nearly anywhere in North America, and not just in the Maritimes? The way the boys act reminds me of some of the ritual courtships of birds and animals. Do you think it continues, in people after marriage?

## LAMENT FOR JAMES TALBOT

This poem is a portrait of a small-town politician. Does the picture of James Talbot seem real to you? Does it seem like a portrait of any present-day politician you might happen to know? There seems to me to be a high good humor about the poem, and Nowlan must have regarded James Talbot with affection. Do you feel the same way? Was he a rascal? Do you think rascals are more lovable than honest and upright men?

## THE GIFT

Why does the Eskimo carving shock the woman in this poem? Should she be shocked? Do you think people who are shocked by such things generally enjoy life very much? If they don't, why not?

## NANCY

Do we ever know someone other than ourselves really well, such as Nowlan appears to know Nancy? Do you think this poem is a memory of childhood? Was Nancy much more than just a girl (if a girl is ever just a girl) in Nowlan's mind?

## STREET CORNER IDLER

Do you think what Nowlan means in this poem is that bums and tramps don't know what they want anymore? Did they ever know? Do you think the idler mentioned has enough to eat? Is there any connection between the sort of street corner idler Nowlan is talking about and the tramps of the great Depression? Would you expect someone to be grateful if you gave him something to eat?

## I KNEW THE SEASONS ERE I KNEW THE HOURS

Judged on the basis of this poem, do you think Nowlan had a happy childhood? Are your own memories of pre-school days equally vivid? Do you have memories of your own that occur to you once in a while? Do you think mostly of the past, present or future?

## THE BULL MOOSE

Do you think it was really necessary to kill the moose in this poem? Couldn't he have been transported back to the woods one way or another? Near the beginning of the poem Nowlan says the cattle were "scenting the musk of death". Do you think anything had happened to the moose before he came to the cattle pasture? Or does Nowlan mean that somehow the cattle sensed that death was approaching in the shape of men and guns? Is this poem religious in any way? If so, why? And why do you think all the young men blew their car horns as the moose died?

### THE EXECUTION

Were you ever accused and punished for something you didn't do? Is that what Nowlan means in this poem? Could it really happen? Do you think the spectators knew the wrong man was being hung or not? Was the wrong man being hung, really?

## *Derek Pethick*

### THE NU NOLLEJ

Of course this is a satire on the forms and methods of modern education. The writer says this particular method didn't work very well, since the students failed exams later. However, should there be exams set at all? Can you think of any way of improving the school system? That's a pretty big question, and there could be some non-serious answers. For instance, right now, are you learning the things you want to learn? Is talking about poems one of the things you want to do? If not, why not? When I went to school part of the method of teaching poetry was to memorize the stuff, and I believe much of the school curriculum today is memory-work. How do you feel about memory-work? What could replace it?

## *A. W. Purdy*

I wrote the next few poems myself, and I don't particularly like asking questions about them (or any poems) which might narrow their meaning. Do you think I should be glad to explain the poems to you since I edited the book? Of course, some things need to be explained, since they are peculiar to a particular period of time and circumstances.

## OLD ALEX

Old Alex wasn't a very likeable character in any sense. He retired from business some twenty years ago, when he was about seventy years of age. Alex had little money, but did own a house, and this he traded to another man in return for bed and board for as long as he lived. Alex was an extreme character, and one couldn't possibly be neutral about him. And of course, I wasn't. But he did inspire me with a kind of awe at his nastiness, the same feeling I might have for a volcano that might spew me with lava or an H-bomb that might seem very beautiful before it killed me. I admired Alex—in a queer way. Can you admire him? Can you ever admire a murderer, or someone like Hitler? Do you think meanness in other people ever gives one a "holier than thou" feeling? Do you ever try to imagine how other people feel if they dislike you? How could they possibly dislike you? Perhaps one can figure out reasons for their dislike, but rarely for their possible love. Do you think that's true? Is either love or dislike more logical than the other? Do you feel the same way as I did about Alex? Or is it only a poem? So what is a poem?

## PERCY LAWSON

From 1950 to 1955 I worked in a mattress factory in Vancouver. A friend and myself decided that conditions were not exactly ideal, therefore we introduced a labour union into the factory. I had more seniority than the other workers so they made me shop steward and their representative at wage negotiations—a job I didn't particularly want or like. During wage negotiations I sat there in the boss's office feeling nervous, out of place and a little scared. Would you feel that way in a similar situation? Percy Lawson was a veteran labour organizer and negotiator with the nerve of a burglar. The time I'm talking about in this poem was after the union had been in for some time; we had already received the first wage agreement and were now negotiating the second one. Watt was the factory manager, the "boss". If I have used his right name (I have, by the way) do you think I've given him grounds to sue me for libel? Do you think I was right to admire Lawson, or, he being a veteran labour negotiator, did he deserve any admiration? Does working for years and years in a factory seem to you a wasted lifetime, as it did to me?

## HOCKEY PLAYERS

When I wrote this poem I used a strong rhythmic meter for two sections of it, the rest being fairly prosey. I know why I did that, but can you think of a reason? Or do you see two different rhythms? It might be that I just imagined I wrote in two rhythms. Do you think the poem is an accurate description of hockey players in Canada, as far as it goes? I suppose what I'm saying is that there must be a feeling of intoxication and delight in the players themselves that comes from being highly skilled at a difficult game. Would money have anything to do with the players' enjoyment? There are always people who are not good at games, who never behave naturally with other people. Is it their own fault? Do you feel sorry for them? How do you feel about these "outsiders" generally?

## ABOUT BEING A MEMBER OF OUR ARMED FORCES

Some terms in this poem require explanation. For instance, "zombies" were the conscripts in the last war and the C.W.A.C.'s was the Canadian Women's Army Corps. At the war's beginning the armed forces were short of real shoot-em-dead rifles and had to use wooden ones for drilling purposes. How do you feel about me in this poem—was I stupid or just someone trapped in a war? Have you ever been trapped by something, no matter what? Is it possible to be so closely involved in an event that you have very little feeling about it? Do you think that wars are everyone's fault, or the fault of a particular group of people? Or are they anyone's fault?

## INTERRUPTION

The events in this poem did happen. The new house was built, the various wild creatures did do all the things described. And yet the effects of the poem seems to me, the writer, to be partly fantasy. I suppose the imagery does that. Mice didn't really touch one of my thoughts, but we know so little about extra sensory perception that it may not be unreasonable to suppose they sensed, felt, or smelled a man sleeping nearby. I have also the feeling that the events in this poem happened a long time ago, although it was only a few years ago.

Do you feel anything similar to the way I do about that? I mean, you look back at the events of your own past, and they are curiously static, immovable, fixed in time. You can change nothing, although the way you think of things may alter, or your memory restore forgotten things that happened. But whatever actions you make now, anything at all, alter your own future as well as the future of others. It seems an odd thought to me that a house built where there was no house before changes the habits of animals. Would you feel any responsibility in similar circumstances? Should I, for instance, feel responsibility over the dead robins and drowned chipmunk?

### THE DRUNK TANK

There is a key phrase in this poem that is repeated three times. Can you pick it out without looking back at the poem? What do you interpret this phrase as meaning? Do you think the man being described by the speaker is quite normal and that you might react the same way in his shoes? What about the other man—the speaker—does he seem normal to you? How would you explain the inconsistencies in the poem, such as the first man believing the second man is his friend, but the second man denying he knows the first? Do you think the poem tries to say anything about human character? The difficulty of communication? Anything?

## *James Reaney*

### KLAXON

In the early part of this poem it sounds as if cars have taken over the world. At the end of the poem the situation is reversed, nobody will drive cars any more, everyone "wished to walk." Could a situation like this ever really come about? Of course, Reaney is exaggerating when he says cars begged for masters. Compare the attitude towards cars here with Alden Nowlan's "Saturday Night."

# *Joe Rosenblatt*

## WAITER THERE'S AN ALLIGATOR IN MY COFFEE

What meaning is Rosenblatt trying to get across in this poem, if any? Does the poem seem absurd to you? Do you think the writer meant it to be absurd?

## THE WORK SHIFT

Why should Christ have worn the work boots in question along the road to Golgotha? Do you think Rosenblatt is right when he says "the only difference/between me and that family/is that I take a longer road to hell"? What is meant by "J. Edgaring eyes"? If we understand this term now, it's not likely to be understood ten or twenty years from now. Do you think poems should be written so that their meaning is clear in a hundred years, or only ten or twenty years?

# *W.W.E. Ross*

## APOLOGIES TO ROBERT FROST

This poem is a pastiche, an imitation of the writing style of the American poet Robert Frost. But when you read this imitation, it's liable to make you smile or laugh. Whereas, when you read Frost, you're liable to take him quite seriously. Why the difference in the reader's reactions? Does this discursive, and wordy style amuse you? Again, how can Ross's poem be funny and Frost's serious, when they are almost the same? If you didn't know this poem was an imitation of Frost would it still be funny? There is a point made at the end, which is almost a commentary on one of Canada's Prime Ministers (Mackenzie King) political methods: wait till what's unusual goes away. In other words do nothing and the problem will disappear or change into something else. Do you think that's a valid course of non-action in a Prime Minister or anyone else?

# *Duncan Campbell Scott*

## THE FORSAKEN

Among the Indians and Eskimos today do you think an old woman would ever be abandoned like this and left to die? Do you think Indians in Canada live long and happy lives and are treated justly? Do you admire the old woman in this poem? What were the reasons for her abandonment? Was it really necessary?

# *F. R. Scott*

## EXAMINER

Do you see yourself as a 'hot and discouraged youth' sometimes? In other words, is this a true picture of an examination? Do you think the examiner plots your downfall, or is the writer only being humourous? Scott has an attitude towards formal education in this poem. How would you identify this attitude? He compares the 'professional mowers' altering nature into sameness with what is being done to students by 'modern' educatonal methods. Do you think it's a valid comparison? Do you resent having to reach 'page 10 by Tuesday'? In my view, this poem deals with the fundamental idea that the culture we are born into shapes us into persons who very much resemble all other persons. Few of us like that process. What interests me is not necessarily of interest to you, and vice-versa. Most of us want to be individuals, be ourselves, whatever that may be. Is it still possible to be 'yourself'?

## LAURENTIAN SHIELD

After having ignored it for many years, Canadians have a new interest in the Arctic. Do you think it may be possible in the future to develop the north in the way Scott suggests? The poem amounts to a prediction, and in it northern development seems just a matter of time. Do you think this development is a job that must be done for the good of the country? Or does it really matter very much?

# *Robert Service*

## FIVE-PER-CENT

If you know Service's "Songs of a Sourdough" and other poems about the Yukon, you might think he had never written anything else. I had never seen this poem until I started reading everything I could, looking for poems for this book. Do you think the attitude of the speaker in this poem amounts to hypocrisy, and he may admire the working man but doesn't really want to be one himself? Have you seen such an attitude in other people? On the other hand, it might not be hypocrisy, it could very well be a satire on rich and wealthy people who have other people to do their work for them. Which is it, hypocrisy or satire, or both?

# *A. J. M. Smith*

## THE LONELY LAND

This is a very well-known poem, and has been taken by many to be a very accurate portrait of Canada. But is it really? Isn't Canada, with a population of twenty million strung just north of the U.S. border, now principally urban in population. Of course, Smith is talking about wilderness land. Is it a good description of these areas? Can strength really be broken by strength and remain strong? If so, can you think of any examples of this phenomenon?

## TO HOLD IN A POEM

Smith has two things in this poem that he seems to have much affection for. What are they? Can one really hold the many and various qualities of a country "in a poem of words"? Is the "spirit of prairie and river" austere? Do you yourself regard Canada as "The North"? When Smith calls the country "unbuyable," do you suppose he has in mind the 65% figure of Canadian industry held by foreign owners?

# *Raymond Souster*

## FLIGHT OF THE ROLLER-COASTER

Raymond Souster has written about Toronto, its downtown streets and slums and people, for nearly all his life. He has finally achieved the appellation of "Toronto Poet." He is identified with a particular place and time, and there is little doubt that he'll live out his life and write more poems about Toronto. Raymond Souster was a member of the R.C.A.F. during the war, and has been a bank employee for the twenty some years since.

What sort of mood do you see in this poem? Of course, it's fantasy, but is that all? Is there any contrast to the actions of the roller-coaster and the people of the amusement park? The whole thing is slightly reminiscent of flying saucers to me, and other weird and wonderful occurrences. Have you ever personally seen things or felt things you couldn't explain? Did you mention them to a friend or some other person who disbelieved you? One is liable to say: well, roller-coasters can't head off into the clouds like that, but it might be nice if they did—if once in a while unusual things, charming things, crazy things, actually did happen. Do you ever feel that way?

## THE VICTORY

Souster's treatment of bums and skid-row derelicts is a mixture of pity, compassion, and I believe slight contempt. Of course, he would deny that last word. Okay, what do you make of the race between the hand and the machine here to reach the cigarette butt? The implications of this poem, like most of Souster's, could be expanded to a length of several pages. If a prime quality of poetry is condensation, then Souster is almost without equal in this respect. What does the "age-old, human smile/of victory" mean?

## THE TOP HAT

Here's another in Souster's gallery of Toronto people. Should we call such people "characters" and smile at them indulgently? Would you find it refreshing to see an old man wearing a top-hat on Bay Street, Toronto? If you were in Yorkville, you would see far more incongruous and outlandish apparel than that. He walked as if "the whole/damn street belonged to him"—Why should that be so engaging and ingratiating to Souster?

## THE INTRODUCTION

What is the difference between what we are doing here with these questions of mine and what Souster is talking about in his poem? Or is there a difference?

## LAKE OF BAYS

Have you seen things like this happen, or been involved in them yourself? You are pushed into a situation where you must take a chance, take a dare, do something risky, else you will lose face or seem afraid? Was Souster's mother right when she said the girl would never grow up to be a lady? What is a lady? If a girl, are you a lady or do you want to be one later? Why will Souster remember this girl?

## WHEN IT COMES MY TURN

Would your thoughts about death be the same as Souster's? Or have you thought much about death? Does your ambition cause you to reach for the sun or do you settle for something less, something more within reach? Is the largest ambition the only thing worth reaching for? Does one have to make a choice between the largest and smallest of one's ambitions?

## THE BURIAL

Souster mentions the ten thousand deaths of slaughter-house animals as against this one death of a young girl. Does he mean the animals' or the girl's death is less important? Or does he mean either? Did Souster's feeling so alive have anything to do with his being at this funeral? Why did he want the sun to shine down and warm the girl's face? Do you think he knew the girl personally and felt some affection for her? Why should he mention her in that often-used phrase, as being "so young to die"? Whatever our age is, aren't we all too young to die? What has age really got to do with it?

## THIS WIND

Why does Souster associate the wind with so many different things at different times? Would you associate a wind with lilacs and a girl's touch? How do you think Souster was feeling when he wrote this poem? Is he actually right about the wind of December being the same wind that will come in spring?

## FREEZE UP

Have you ever really been able to identify the exact instant when anything happened? What things? I suppose we all have presentiments that things are about to happen, or not to happen. Is that our imagination at work? Could the waterfall know when it couldn't budge? Do you find it interesting to speculate on the idea that a drop of water went over a waterfall, then another came and froze instead of going over? When was the exact instant you realized there were other countries besides Canada, or that red was a colour, or that girls were different, and life was either good or bad or both?

## SOMEONE HAS TO EAT

Does someone really have to eat the stale food Souster is talking about here? Is that the way life is, the way the world is? Why does Souster call these people "children of the shadows"? Do you ever feel pity, passion or contempt for the people who eat such food? Thousands of people starve to death, die of malnutrition, in the world every year. How do you feel about that?

## SETTING THE TRAP

Do you regard killing animals that are an annoyance and a bother to people as cruelty? Was the man Souster is talking about really a good man? Why would he curse if there isn't one dead animal in the morning? If we regard killing animals as cruelty and dislike it, do you think any of us ought to sleep soundly if we are not guilty of such cruelty? Are there other things we might regard as cruelty that we have committed? What is the worst thing you think human beings can do? Name a few. How many have you committed yourself? Do you feel guilty about them? If you did you might not sleep well, therefore doesn't one have to draw a dividing line between what cruelty is important and what isn't? Or is all cruelty important?

## *Francis Sparshott*

### NEANDERTHAL NATIONAL ANTHEM

No one can possibly understand this poem if they do not know that Neanderthal Man, Java Man, Sinanthropus and Proconsul are fossilized remnants of human and sub-human remains—many thousands of years old. Piltdown Man was thought to be another of these fossil man discoveries, but later turned out to be a fake perpetrated by a man named Dawson for reasons unknown. What does Sparshott mean by the "old Darwinian cause"? Do you think there's any hint of racialism or snobbery in this poem? If so, could it be a parody on our modern selves? Why did they all get up and run when Homo Sapiens came along?

## *Peter Stevens*

### WARMING UP, TUNING IN

What is this poem all about? Who are the "grey phantoms" who carry "fire on their backs"? How does the "Cain-mark" of the first line connect up with the "silver-livid flame" of the last line? Why do the walls "ooze like thick glue/slipping shapeless round me"? Why do the writer's children "weep by the burning huts"? Would you say the writer is involved in what he describes? Or is he an observer?

## *A. Szumigalski*

### VICTIM

This poem is definitely a fantasy, but elements of reality stick out of it here and there. Can you identify what you think is fantasy and what might be reality? Is the scene itself real, or does it all happen in someone's mind? How old is the girl? Could the whole thing be a photograph? Do you think the writer is deliberately trying to puzzle his readers? Or is he describing a scene where each of the characters knows only part of what actually happened? Do most people sob and beat their breasts when they find a dead body? Is there any affection shown in the poem?

## *Ian Tyson*

### FOUR STRONG WINDS

This song concerns a basic human loneliness, the need of one person for another and circumstances that often make it impossible for them to be together. Specifically, it's also about the wandering migratory workers of Canada, the unskilled harvest hands of the Thirties, tobacco workers at Delhi, the men who take temporary jobs in mine, mill or factory, then quit or get fired and blow all their money on whisky or a woman or both. It's about the wanderers by road and rail, the outsiders, the down-and-outers, the losers.

The young guy in this song-poem had such a temporary job and found such a girl. He hadn't anticipated falling in love with her but he did. Both man and girl knew the affair must end, and seem to take this ending for granted before it actually happens. It had to end because of tough unyielding circumstances (economic), perhaps also because the man's character was affected by his wandering life and he can't settle down; also because of the way things are, the way people are.

It's a sad and sentimental song, one of the very few I've heard that sounds absolutely authentic. Sure, it happens all the time, the little personal tragedies that tear your guts out; it's happening now. In the Hungry Thirties, riding the freight trains myself, I saw hundreds of such guys as the one in the song. They didn't tell me their stories, but unless they had no insides most of them had left a girl somewhere behind and might easily have said "I'll look for you if I'm ever back this way".

How about it—am I right when I say that's what the song is all about? Do you think the man shouldn't have given up so easily, and he really should have sent the girl money to meet him in Alberta "where there's work there in the fall"? Would you do the same as he did? If you're a girl, and it happened to you, would you remember such a man? Is that the way life is—that we're all defeated by something, and there is no hope for a good life? Tyson's "Four Strong Winds" and "seven seas" signify the fates for me, the destiny you can't wriggle out of—There's a precedent for them in Greek tragedy. Do you think a person can change his own fate and destiny?

# *Tom Wayman*

## THE DOW RECRUITER, or
## This Young Man Is Making Up His Mind

This poem relates to student riots at Canadian universities in the late sixties when agents of various chemical companies came to offer employment to soon-to-be-graduated students. The speaker in the poem is the Dow recruiter. The difficulties of his job seem similar, perhaps, to difficulties connected with other people's jobs. He might talk them over with his wife after work sometimes. If you were such a man, how would you explain the whole business to your wife? I mean: would you justify yourself; or would you say somebody has to do such jobs and obey orders while doing them? Or would you feel miserable because the company you worked for, whatever its name, sold chemicals for use in a war? The red flowers along the lane outside the recruiter's house are compared to a man. Why does the writer make this comparison? There is a strong contrast made between the recruiter's quiet house and the violence of his daily work, shouting students and red-faced officials. What does the writer want to show by this contrast? What do you feel is the basic subject of the poem?

## THE SEASON OF EDEN

Do you think the "fifteen winds" mentioned in the poem are a Biblical myth, or something the author has invented? I don't know which myself, and am not sure it's a good idea to find out. What is meant by "the necessary crash of sweat"? After that, apparently these mythic or invented winds stop touching a girl. A delicate thought, but is it true?

# *Ian Young*

## FEAR OF THE LANDSCAPE

A landscape is described in this poem. Do you think it's a perfectly ordinary landscape, a place any of us might wander into? Does anything happen in the poem to make you think the landscape might not be ordinary? As a comparison, in De la Mare's "The Listeners" an eerie, ghost-haunted scene is described. Is this landscape at all similar to De la Mare's? Assuming that the scene in this poem produces an odd feeling in the reader, how does the writer do this? Silence is emphasized in the poem. Why?